OECD INSIGHTS

From Crisis to Recovery

*The Causes, Course and Consequences
of the Great Recession*

Brian Keeley and Patrick Love

OECD

ORGANISATION FOR ECONOMIC CO-OPERATION AND DEVELOPMENT

The OECD is a unique forum where the governments of 32 democracies work together to address the economic, social and environmental challenges of globalisation. The OECD is also at the forefront of efforts to understand and to help governments respond to new developments and concerns, such as corporate governance, the information economy and the challenges of an ageing population. The Organisation provides a setting where governments can compare policy experiences, seek answers to common problems, identify good practice and work to co-ordinate domestic and international policies.

The OECD member countries are: Australia, Austria, Belgium, Canada, Chile, the Czech Republic, Denmark, Finland, France, Germany, Greece, Hungary, Iceland, Ireland, Italy, Japan, Korea, Luxembourg, Mexico, the Netherlands, New Zealand, Norway, Poland, Portugal, the Slovak Republic, Slovenia, Spain, Sweden, Switzerland, Turkey, the United Kingdom and the United States. The Commission of the European Communities takes part in the work of the OECD.

The opinions expressed and arguments employed herein do not necessarily reflect the official views of the OECD member countries.

Series: OECD Insights
ISSN: 1993-6745 (print)
ISSN: 1993-6753 (on line)

ISBN: 978-92-64-06911-4 (print)
ISBN: 978-92-64-07707-2 (on line)

Foreword

The current global economic crisis was triggered by a financial crisis caused by ever-increasing thirst for short-term profit. In addition, against a background of government support for the expansion of financial markets, many people turned a blind eye to basic issues of business ethics and regulation. We now need to rewrite the rules of finance and global business. To restore the trust that is fundamental to functioning markets, we need better regulation, better supervision, better corporate governance and better co-ordination.

We also need fairer social policies and an end to the bottlenecks that block competition and innovation and hamper sustainable growth. We must also find the most productive ways for governments to exit from their massive emergency interventions once the world economy is firmly back on a growth path.

Dealing with fiscal deficits and unemployment while encouraging new sources of growth will absorb policy makers' attention in the near term, but lifting our collective sights to focus on wider issues, such as the environment and development, is a challenge we must also meet.

How can we move from recession to recovery? The OECD's strategic response involves strengthening corporate governance and doing more to combat the dark sides of globalisation, such as corruption and tax evasion.

As well as correcting the mistakes of the past, we have to prepare the future. We are elaborating a "Green Growth Strategy" to guide national and international policies so that all countries can realise the potential of this new approach to growth. Our analysis shows a need for governments to take a stronger lead in fostering greener production, procurement and consumption patterns by devising clearer frameworks and ensuring that markets work properly. They should drop some costly habits too, notably subsidising fossil fuels, which would help fight climate change and save money as well.

We also need new thinking in other areas, from competition, investment and pensions policies to tackling education, health care, social exclusion and poverty. We need to raise productivity while keeping trade and investment frontiers open. We must find ways to spread opportunity and the fruits of future growth more evenly and encourage the scientific, technical and organisational innovation needed for a "green" recovery.

This latest *Insights* book draws on the OECD's analyses of why the financial crisis occurred and how it spread so rapidly into the real economy. It calls on the Organisation's extensive expertise in the analysis of economic growth, employment policy, financial markets and the other domains affected by the crisis and crucial to the recovery.

I trust you will find it useful in understanding the origins of our present situation and in judging the responses to it.

Angel Gurría

Secretary General to the OECD

Acknowledgements

The authors very gratefully acknowledge the advice and assistance of Pablo Antolin, Andrew Auerbach, Tim Besley, Sveinbjörn Blöndal, Adrian Blundell-Wignall, Rory Clarke, Emmanuel Dalmenesche, Jean-Christophe Dumont, Carolyn Ervin, Alessandro Goglio, Johannes Jütting, Katherine Kraig-Ernandes, Andrew Mold, Lynn Robertson, Stéfanie Payet, Glenda Quintini, Jean-Marc Salou, Stefano Scarpetta, Paul Swaim, David Turner, Jane Voros, Gert Wehinger, Juan Yermo and William R. White.

Currency note

Currency references are in US dollars unless otherwise indicated.

OECD Insights is a series of primers commissioned by the OECD Public Affairs and Communication Directorate. They draw on the Organisation's research and expertise to introduce and explain some of today's most pressing social and economic issues to non-specialist readers.

CONTENTS

This book has...

StatLinks

A service that delivers Excel® files from the printed page!

Look for the *StatLinks* at the bottom right-hand corner of the tables or graphs in this book. To download the matching Excel® spreadsheet, just type the link into your Internet browser, starting with the *http://dx.doi.org* prefix.

If you're reading the PDF e-book edition, and your PC is connected to the Internet, simply click on the link. You'll find *StatLinks* appearing in more OECD books.

Introduction

The financial crisis of late 2008 was the spark for the most serious economic slowdown since World War II. The Great Recession, as some have called it, will continue to overshadow economies for years to come through legacies such as unemployment and public debt.

By way of introduction …

Sometime in the early 2000s, Clarence Nathan took out a loan. He wasn't in full-time employment but held down three part-time jobs, none of them very secure, and earned about $45 000 a year. Even Mr. Nathan was surprised anyone would give him a loan against his house, especially a sum like $540 000.

"I wouldn't have loaned me the money," he later told National Public Radio in the United States. "And nobody that I know would have loaned me the money. I know guys who are criminals who wouldn't loan me that and they break your knee-caps. I don't know why the bank did it. I'm serious … $540 000 to a person with bad credit."

Why did the bank do it? On the face of it, the bank's decision made no sense. Indeed, if Mr. Nathan had applied for such a loan ten years earlier, he wouldn't have got it. But in the intervening period, a couple of things changed. The first was that borrowing in the United States and other countries became, and stayed, relatively cheap, buoyed by vast inflows from emerging economies like China. In essence, there was a huge pool of money just waiting to be lent.

The other thing that changed was the banks themselves. They became ever more eager to take big risks, in the expectation of making big returns. Except, as far as the banks were concerned, they weren't really taking risks. Thanks to clever financial innovations, they were able to slice and dice loans such as Mr. Nathan's into so many tiny parts that even if he defaulted (which he did) the loss would be spread out so widely that no one would really feel it. Better still for the bank, it would have sold off the loan to someone else long before Mr. Nathan experienced any problems. And if he couldn't meet his debts, he could always sell his house at a profit – after all, there had been no nationwide decline in house prices in the United States since the 1930s.

For a time, it seemed, risk had become so well managed that it just wasn't as, well, risky as it used to be. It made sense both to lend and to borrow, and so pretty much everyone did. In 2005, homeowners in the US borrowed $750 billion against the value of their homes – about seven times more than a decade earlier. After all, what could go wrong ….

Pop!

By this stage, you either know or have guessed the answer: the bubble burst. Not for the first time, "irrational exuberance" banged up against hard reality, and hard reality won. It usually does.

The resulting financial carnage was exemplified by the collapse of Lehman Brothers in September 2008, even though the crisis had been brewing for a long time before then. What started as a financial crisis quickly made its way into the "real economy", triggering an unprecedented collapse in world trade, widespread job losses and the first contraction in the global economy since the Second World War. No wonder some people called it the "Great Recession".

This book is about that crisis, the subsequent downturn and the prospects for strong recovery. It examines the roots of the crisis, how it spread into the real economy, and the ways in which the aftershocks of the Great Recession will continue to be felt for years to come.

The recession and its legacies

Economic memories are often short, which is one reason, perhaps, why financial crises and bubbles tend to recur with such frequency. Spotting the factors in advance that may be leading up to such events is not easy (if it were, they wouldn't occur). But at bottom, one mistaken notion tends to crop up repeatedly: a sense that, for some reason or other, the old rules of economies and financial markets no longer apply. Sometimes the rules do indeed change, but as often as not they do not. As the noted investor and businessman Sir John Templeton once remarked, "The four most dangerous words in investing are, 'this time it's different'."

As it turned out, this time wasn't different: risk wasn't nearly as well managed as people thought it was. Indeed, it had only been deepened, both by the huge imbalances that emerged in the global economy in recent decades and by the sea change that swept over financial institutions. And, just as in the past, a financial crisis had a huge impact on the real economy – the world in which most of us earn our living.

"Even if the crisis did not lead – to paraphrase a pop hit of a few years ago – to the 'end of the world as we know it', there is at least agreement that it was more than just one of those turbulences that economies occasionally experience."

OECD Factbook 2010

What *was* different was the magnitude of the crisis and how synchronised it was: this wasn't just a regional event, like the Asian financial downturn of the late 1990s, but a global crisis, at least in its onset. The numbers are striking. According to estimates by the World Bank, the total world economy contracted by 2.1% in 2009 – an unprecedented fall in the post-war era. In the OECD area, there was an economic contraction of 4.7% between the first quarter of 2008 and the second quarter of 2009. A plunge in global trade was another sign of the seriousness of the crisis. Worldwide, the volume of world trade in goods and services fell by 12% in 2009, according to the WTO.

Unemployment rose sharply, reaching a post-war record of 8.7% in the OECD area – that meant an extra 17 million people were out of work by early 2010 compared with two years earlier. The situation became – and remains – especially serious for young people: in the OECD area, the employment rate for young people (15-24 year-olds) fell by more than 8 percentage points. In countries like France and Italy, about one in four young people are unemployed, while in Spain it's more than two in five. Job creation traditionally lags recovery, so even if economies rebound strongly, high rates of unemployment won't vanish for some time yet.

Another legacy of the recession is debt. Governments borrowed heavily during the crisis to keep financial institutions afloat and to stimulate activity. By 2011, government debt in OECD countries will typically be equal to about 100% of GDP – in other words, the value of their total output of goods and services.

That action was necessary, but it had the effect of transferring the financial crisis from the private sector to the public sector. In the initial phase of the crisis, financial institutions were "overleveraged" – in effect, they couldn't meet their debts. Rescuing them, and the wider economy, shifted the problem on to governments, leaving them with high levels of debt. This has already created major challenges for countries like Greece and Spain and put pressure on the euro. In coming years, the need to reduce such borrowings will confront societies across the OECD area with some tough choices on how best to balance taxation with spending, and where best to direct resources in order to generate long-term prosperity.

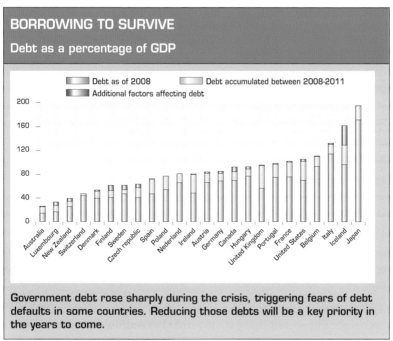

BORROWING TO SURVIVE

Debt as a percentage of GDP

Debt as of 2008 | Debt accumulated between 2008-2011
Additional factors affecting debt

Government debt rose sharply during the crisis, triggering fears of debt defaults in some countries. Reducing those debts will be a key priority in the years to come.

Source: OECD Factbook 2010.

StatLink http://dx.doi.org/10.1787/888932320523

What this book is about ...

Trying to predict where the global economy might go next has proved to be one of the toughest challenges of the crisis. Just as the speed and suddenness of the crisis's onset caught most people unawares, the subsequent course of the recession and recovery has sprung more surprises than a Hollywood thriller. Predictions of economic collapse in the depths of the crisis were probably overstated. But, equally, forecasts of a rapid recovery look to have been wide of the mark.

What does seem clear is that the synchronised plunge that marked the start of the crisis was not mirrored at the other end by a simultaneous rebound. Countries emerged from recession, but the pace of their recovery varied. Emerging economies, especially in Asia, bounced back strongly, while some low-income countries did much better than many would have expected. Among the developed economies of the OECD area, however, the picture has been more mixed. Recovery looks set to be sluggish for some time yet, which will only add to the challenge of tackling issues like unemployment and mounting deficits and debts.

> **"The pace of recovery is uneven, and in the US and much of Europe, growth will be too sluggish to make sizeable inroads into the number of unemployed this year."**
>
> Angel Gurría, OECD Secretary-General, speech in Prague, April 2010

Challenges such as those have come to figure ever more prominently on the agenda of the OECD. Just like governments, other intergovernmental organisations, businesses and citizens, the OECD has had to respond to a fast-moving economic situation since the crisis broke. Its efforts have revolved around three main axes, which can be summed up under the challenge of building a **stronger**, **cleaner**, **fairer** world economy: a stronger economy is one that produces sustainable growth, uses appropriate regulation to build resilience to crises and makes the most of its workforce. A cleaner economy is "greener", but cleaner, too, in the sense of combating bribery, corruption and tax evasion. And a fairer economy is one that provides people with opportunities regardless of their background and that delivers improved living standards to the world's poorest people.

This book reflects those efforts. To give the necessary context to what follows, it begins by tracing the causes and course of the crisis. It then goes on to look at the post-crisis challenges our economies and societies face in a number of areas, including employment, pensions and financial regulation. By necessity, this book can present only a limited overview, but it provides ways in which readers can delve deeper. In each chapter there are graphics and charts from OECD publications and papers as well as direct quotations from their texts. At the end of each chapter, there's a section offering pointers to further information and reading from the OECD, and links to other intergovernmental bodies and information sources.

Chapter 2 looks at the roots of the financial crisis, including how techniques like securitisation greatly increased the vulnerability of banks to failure.

Chapter 3 examines the routes of the recession – how a financial crisis morphed into a crisis for the global economy.

Chapter 4 looks at the impact on jobs, including the risk that the recession will be followed by a jobless recovery that contributes to a "lost generation" of young people in the workforce.

Chapter 5 looks at the impact on pensions: the crisis highlighted issues in both funding and benefits that population ageing and changing career patterns could aggravate.

Chapter 6 considers the push for new rules and standards in three key areas – financial markets, tax evasion and business and economic ethics.

Finally, **Chapter 7** examines some longer-term issues arising from the recession, including rising national debts, the prospects for turning the recovery into an opportunity for "green growth" and the challenges facing economics as a profession.

What is the OECD?

The Organisation for Economic Co-operation and Development, or OECD, brings together leading industrialised countries committed to democracy and the market economy to tackle key economic, social and governance challenges in the globalised world economy. As of 2008, its members accounted for 60% of the world's trade and close to 70% of the world's Gross National Income, or GNI (a measure of countries' economic performance).

The OECD traces its roots back to the Marshall Plan that rebuilt Europe after World War II. The mission then was to work towards sustainable economic growth and employment and to raise people's living standards. These remain core goals of the OECD. The organisation also works to build sound economic growth, both for member countries and those in the developing world, and seeks to help the development of non-discriminatory global trade. With that in mind, the OECD has forged links with many of the world's emerging economies and shares expertise and exchanges views with more than 100 other countries and economies around the world.

In recent years, the OECD has also begun a process of enlargement, inviting a number of countries to open talks on joining the organisation's existing members. Four of those – Chile, Estonia, Israel and Slovenia – were invited to join in 2010, while talks continue with a fifth country, Russia. In addition, the OECD has also begun a process of enhanced engagement with five emerging economies – Brazil, China, India, Indonesia and South Africa.

Numbers play a key role in the OECD's work, constantly informing the organisation's evidence-based policy advice. The organisation is one of the world's leading sources for comparable data on subjects ranging from economic indicators to education and health. These data play a key role in helping member governments to compare their policy experiences. The OECD also produces guidelines, recommendations and templates for international co-operation on areas such as taxation and technical issues that are essential for countries to make progress in the globalising economy.

www.oecd.org

2

The suddenness of the financial crisis caught many unawares. In reality, financial pressures had been building for years as funds flooded from emerging economies like China to developed economies like the US. This was exacerbated by banks' increasingly reckless taste for risk.

The Roots of a Crisis

By way of introduction...

The events of 2008 have already passed into history, but they still have the power to take our breath away. Over a matter of months, a succession of earthquakes struck the world's financial system – the sort of events that might normally happen only once in a century.

In reality, the warning signs were already there in 2007, when severe pressure began building in the subprime securities market. Then, in March 2008, the investment bank and brokerage Bear Stearns collapsed. More was to come. Early in September, the US government announced it was taking control of Fannie Mae and Freddie Mac, two huge entities that underpin mortgage lending in the United States. Then, in the middle of that month, came news of the collapse of investment bank Lehman Brothers. A fixture on Wall Street, Lehman had been a home to the sort of traders and dealers that novelist Tom Wolfe once dubbed "masters of the universe". Around the same time, another of Wall Street's legends, Merrill Lynch, avoided Lehman's fate only by selling itself to the Bank of America.

It wasn't just investment banks that found themselves in trouble. The biggest insurer in the US, American Insurance Group (AIG), teetered on the brink of failure due to bad bets it had made on insuring complex financial securities. It survived only after billions of dollars of bailouts from Washington.

How did the stock markets react? In New York, the Dow Jones Index fell 777 points on 29 September, its biggest-ever one-day fall. That was a mirror of wider fears that the world's financial system was on the brink of meltdown. The mood was summed up on the cover of *The Economist*, not usually given to panic, which depicted a man standing on the edge of a crumbling cliff accompanied by the headline, "World on the edge".

▶ What happened? Why was the world financial system plunged apparently so suddenly into what many feared at the time would become a crisis to rival the Great Depression? This chapter looks at the pressure that built up in global finance in the years before the crisis struck, and the ways in which new approaches to banking greatly amplified those pressures.

The dam breaks

So, what were the roots of this crisis? One way of answering that question is in terms of a metaphor – an overflowing dam.

The water behind the dam was a **global liquidity bubble** – or easy access to cheap borrowing. This resulted from low interest rates in key economies like Japan and the United States and what amounted to huge support for US finances from China. This idea of a supply of easy money might seem rather abstract, but it had a real impact on everyday life. For example, low inflation helped by the huge supply of goods coming out of Asia, low US interest rates and Asian investment in US Treasury securities made mortgages cheap, encouraging buyers to get into the market, fuelling a bubble in house prices. Other assets, like shares, also rose to levels that were going to be hard to sustain over the long term.

With a real dam, channels might be dug to ease the pressure of water. In the financial world, however, the channels only contributed to the problems. These channels were poor regulation, which created incentives for money-making activities that were dangerous and not always well understood. The result was that banks and other financial institutions suffered huge losses on financial gambles that wiped out their capital.

Lehman was perhaps the most notable collapse, but in reality the problems had been brewing for years. A year earlier, in autumn 2007, for instance, Northern Rock became the first British bank in a century and a half to experience a "run" – where fearful depositors race to retrieve their money. The "Rock" had grown quickly to become one of the country's top mortgage lenders, relying on short-term borrowings, and not its customers' deposits, to finance its lending. Around the same time, a number of banks in Germany also received emergency state support. But perhaps it took the collapse of Lehman to really thrust the full scale of the looming crisis into the public's consciousness. Subsequently, the crisis moved far beyond Wall Street and affected economies around the world.

But, to go back to basics, why did the liquidity bubble form – why did the water build up behind the dam? And what happened to regulation that allowed banks to make such dangerous mistakes?

Water in the dam: what caused the liquidity bubble?

Asset price bubbles are not rare in human history. As far back as the 17th century, the Dutch were gripped by "tulip mania", when speculation in tulip bulbs sent prices soaring – according to one estimate, at the height of the mania the price of some bulbs exceeded $100 000 in present-day values. In the 1920s, share prices soared in New York in the run-up to the 1929 Wall Street Crash. Over the next three or four years, they lost almost nine-tenths of their value. It would take until the middle of the 1950s for New York-listed shares to return to their pre-1929 levels. More recently, the "dotcom bubble" of the late 1990s and early 2000s saw a huge run-up in the price of Internet-related shares before they, too, came back down to earth.

By leading to cuts in US interest rates, the crash that followed the dotcom bubble helped lay the ground for the financial crisis. Let's look in greater detail at how that happened, and at some other factors that helped lead to the build-up of water – or credit – behind the dam.

Low US interest rates: Following the collapse of the dotcom bubble, the US Federal Reserve sharply cut interest rates to stimulate the economy. Low interest rates encourage businesses and consumers to borrow, which boosts spending and, thus, economic activity and jobs. A combination of strong jobs growth, low interest rates and policies to encourage zero-equity loans helped drive house prices higher, but also made home loans more available to lower-income households.

Low Japanese interest rates: Japan's central bank set interest rates at 0% in 2001 as the country sought to secure its economic recovery following the "lost decade" of the 1990s. Such low rates made yen borrowing very cheap, and led to the emergence of the so-called yen carry trade. In basic terms, this meant that speculators borrowed yen (at interest rates of virtually 0%) and then bought much higher yielding assets, such as US bonds. This had the effect of pumping money into the US financial system and some others.

The impact of China and sovereign wealth funds: In recent decades China has become an export powerhouse, manufacturing and selling huge quantities of goods overseas but importing and buying much less. The result is a large surplus, much of which is recycled to the United States. Because China chooses to manage its exchange rate, these flows mean that the central bank carries out much of the recycling by accumulating foreign exchange reserves, which are typically invested in US Treasury securities. China is now the biggest investor in these securities, but it is not alone: many Middle Eastern and East Asian countries, including China, operate sovereign wealth funds, which invest national wealth, often overseas. As oil prices boomed in 2007, the value of some of these funds grew greatly, which added yet more liquidity to the emerging global bubble.

Dangerous channels: mounting insecurities

So, the world economy was awash with easy credit, leading to a big run-up in the price of such assets as houses and shares – in effect, a bubble emerged and, like all bubbles, the day would come when it had to burst. That's serious enough, but what made the problem even worse was a failure to adequately regulate the ways banks and financial institutions managed these flows of cheap credit.

One of the most serious issues was an increase in home loans to people with weak credit records – so-called subprime mortgages – which was encouraged by public policy, for example, with the so-called American Dream legislation (see below). It was attractive to financial institutions to buy these mortgages, package them into mortgage securities and then, with the revenue from the up-front fee banked, to pass the risk on to someone else. There were important tax advantages to brokers in this process, and it contributed to the explosive growth of the credit default swap market, which played a large role in the spread of the crisis between financial institutions.

Subprime borrowing	

Getting a mortgage used to involve going through a lengthy inspection process, but in recent years that changed in a number of countries, most notably in the United States. Providing borrowers were willing to pay a higher rate, they could always find someone to give them a mortgage. This included people with weak "credit scores", which are based on an individual's track record in borrowing. A good credit score means a borrower qualifies for a relatively low – or "prime" – interest rate. A bad score means the borrower must pay a higher – or "subprime" – rate.

A solid, proven income used to matter, too, but that also changed. Instead, borrowers could take a "stated income" mortgage (or "liar's loan"), where they stated how much they were earning in the expectation that nobody would check up on them.

Another feature of home lending was adjustable-rate mortgages, or "teaser loans", which attracted borrowers with an initial low rate that would then rise, often quite sharply, after just a few years. Many borrowers, however, reckoned that house prices would rise faster than their loan rates, meaning they could still sell the house for a profit. For lenders, too, the dangers seemed manageable: they got up-front fees from arranging mortgages, and could disperse the risk of loan defaults through mortgage securitisation.

This process of **mortgage securitisation** played a key role in creating the crisis, so it's worth looking in a little more detail at how the process works. A mortgage provides a bank with the promise of future cash flow over a long period of years as the mortgage borrower pays back the loan on his or her home. However, the bank may not want to wait that long, and may opt for a quicker return by creating a **security** or, specifically, a **residential mortgage-backed security**, or RMBS. In simple terms, a security is a contract that can be bought and sold and which gives the holder a stake in a financial asset. When a bank turns a mortgage into a security and then sells it, the purchaser is buying the right to receive that steady cash flow from those mortgage repayments. This purchaser is most often a special purpose vehicle (SPV) that sells notes of different quality to "buy-and-hold" investors like pension funds. The bank, meanwhile, is getting quick fee revenue for doing the deal, and may or may not have obligations to the SPV in the future, depending on contractual details.

However, things can go wrong: if the mortgage holder can no longer make the payments, the promised cash flow won't materialise for the holder of security. Of course, the house can then be repossessed and sold, but if property prices have started to fall the sale price may not be sufficient to cover the size of the mortgage. Because home lending became more widespread over the past decade (for reasons we'll look at in more detail below), the risk of mortgage default grew. Many of the securities became "toxic" to banks that kept commitments to them. Banks became cautious about lending to each other, because it was not clear how big the losses on these securities might be, and whether it was "safe" to be using other institutions as counterparties in interbank and swap markets, so fuelling the credit crunch.

What is an asset-backed security?

The financial crisis unleashed some financial terms not normally heard beyond the walls of Wall Street brokerages into daily conversation. For example, ABS, or asset-backed security: if you understood mortgage securitisation, then you'll easily understand an ABS: it's a security based on a pool of assets, such as mortgage or credit-card debt, that will yield a future cash flow. Some ABSs are even more exotic: in 1997, the rock star David Bowie created "Bowie Bonds", which gave holders rights to receive income from future royalty payments on his recordings.

A brave new world of banking

Why did banks create these securities, and why did they invest in them with what – in retrospect – looks like recklessness? The answers to these questions are complex and often quite technical, but to a large extent they lie in new approaches to regulation that allowed or effectively encouraged banks to change the ways they did business.

To understand why, we need to know how banks work. In very simple terms, when you put money into your account you are effectively lending money to your bank, in return for which the bank pays you interest. Because you can ask for it back at any time, the money you deposit is considered as part of the bank's **liabilities**.

Your money doesn't just sit in the bank: it will be lent to other people, who will pay higher interest rates on their loans than the bank is paying to you. Because such loans will eventually be paid back to the bank, they are considered as part of the bank's **assets**. So, your money flows through your bank as if through swing-doors – in one side and straight out the other.

But what happens if you want your money back? By law, the bank must have a financial cushion it can draw on if it needs to. This is capital or equity, or the money that shareholders or investors put into the bank to set it up in the first place (it sits on the liabilities side of a bank's balance sheet). Traditionally, the need for a bank to adhere to a **capital adequacy requirement** – or a minimum share of capital as a proportion of its loans – limited how much it could lend and, thus, its growth. Banks were usually conservative businesses – investors who bought bank shares expected to hold onto them for a long time, enjoying small but consistent dividends rather than a rapid profit.

In the 1990s, this approach changed. Many banks began increasingly to focus on growth, both for their businesses and for their share prices – and the way they were regulated increasingly allowed them to do so. Previously, banks had earned much of their revenue from the difference between what they paid depositors and what borrowers paid to the banks. That changed, and banks increasingly relied on **trading income**, which is money earned from buying and selling financial instruments, and fees from mortgage securitisation.

This new approach changed the timeframe over which banks expected to earn their money – rather than waiting patiently over the years for interest payments on loans, they increasingly sought "up-front" returns, or quick payments, from fees and from selling financial products. The way banks paid their staff reflected this new focus: the size of bonuses grew in relation to fixed salaries and they were increasingly based on an executive's ability to generate up-front income. Staff were also offered shares and share options, which meant it was in their interest to drive up the share price of the bank by generating quick earnings.

These innovative approaches to banking – relying increasingly on securitisation and on capital market sales – were pursued most avidly by **investment banks**, a class of banks that serves mainly the needs of the corporate world by raising capital, trading securities and assisting in takeovers and acquisitions. In Europe, many regular banks also have investment banking arms. In the United States, there had long been a division in banking, a legacy of the Great Depression. That split was designed in part to prevent contagion risks between high-risk securities businesses, insurance and commercial banking. For instance, if an investment bank organised a share sale by a company that subsequently ran into trouble, its commercial arm might feel compelled to lend to the company, even if such a loan didn't make great financial sense. In the 1990s, the barriers began to fall, most notably with the repeal of the Depression-era Glass-Steagall Act in 1999. The result was that the appetite for risk-taking spread more widely in US banking conglomerates, which ultimately led some of them and their European counterparts to get into severe difficulties.

Making the most of capital

We saw earlier that there are limits on how much a bank can lend: in very basic terms the size of its lending is limited by the size of its capital. But the way this capital adequacy requirement is calculated under the international Basel capital rules is technical and complex – for instance, riskier loans must be matched by more capital. In recent years, however, banks have been able to do more lending without an equivalent expansion in the size of their capital bases. Two developments allowed this to happen:

The **emergence of "originate-to-distribute" banking**: The idea behind originate-to-distribute banking is fairly straightforward, although the means used to put it into practice can be complicated. In simple terms, it means that a bank makes (or "originates") loans, and then finds ways to get them off its books (to "distribute" them) so that it can make more loans without breaking its capital requirements.

One way to do this before the crisis was through the securitisation of mortgages and placement of them in SPVs like **structured investment vehicles** – or SIVs – and collateralised debt obligations, or CDOs (see box on the following page). SIVs were entities created by banks that borrowed cheap in the short term to fund assets that were of a longer-term duration. The SIVs made their money from the spread – or gap – between the cost of their short-term borrowing and the return from the longer-term holdings. Provided the bank did not issue letters of credit and other such facilities of a year or more, these would not be subject to Basel capital rules.

The main downside was this: SIVs constantly had to persuade lenders to continue giving them short-term loans. As the credit crunch hit, these lenders became ever more cautious, and interest rates on such short-term borrowings rose. SIVs also saw falls in the value of their long-term mortgage-backed securities as it became increasingly clear that many of these were built in part on bad loans. So, SIVs were left facing big losses, and it was the banks that created them that were left with the bill for cleaning up the mess.

What is a CDO?

CDOs, or collateralised debt obligations, are a complex investment security built on a pool of underlying assets, such as mortgage-backed securities. Crucially, each CDO is sliced up and sold in "tranches" that pay different interest rates. The safest tranche, usually given a rating of AAA, pays the lowest rate of interest; riskier tranches, rated BBB or less, pay a higher interest rate – in effect, the bigger the risk you're willing to take, the bigger your return. CDOs blew up during the subprime crisis because some of these risky tranches were subsequently packaged up into new CDOs, which were then sliced up into tranches, including "safe" AAA tranches. As mortgage defaults grew, even cautious investors who thought they were making a safe AAA investment found they were left with nothing, or almost nothing. If you'd like to know more about what went wrong with CDOs, Paddy Hirsch of *Marketplace* has an informative and entertaining explanation here:
http://marketplace.publicradio.org/display/web/2008/10/03/cdo.

The switch from Basel I to Basel II: The size of banks' minimum capital requirements are governed by an international agreement, the 1988 Basel Accord (or "Basel I"), overseen by the Swiss-based Bank for International Settlements (BIS). As banking and finance evolved throughout the 1990s and into this century, the need was seen for a new agreement, which led to the publication of proposals for a "Basel II" accord in 2004.

These accords are highly technical, and their impact on the development of banking practices – as well as their role in fuelling the crisis – is still a matter of debate. Nevertheless, two points are worth noting. First, Basel II effectively regarded routine mortgage lending as less risky than its predecessor did, which allowed banks to issue more mortgages without affecting their capital adequacy requirements. Second, and as a consequence, it made sense for banks in the transition from Basel I to Basel II to move existing mortgages off their balance sheets by way of such methods as mortgage securitisation; they would then be able to take early advantage of the new and more attractive arrangements for mortgage lending laid out in Basel II.

FEELING SECURE?

The explosion of securitisation in the US ($ billion)

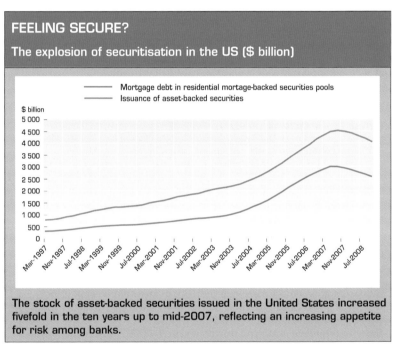

The stock of asset-backed securities issued in the United States increased fivefold in the ten years up to mid-2007, reflecting an increasing appetite for risk among banks.

Source: OECD Factbook 2010.

StatLink ⟨⟨⟨⟨ *http://dx.doi.org/10.1787/888932320542*

Making the most of tax

Another great attraction of the securitisation model was the ability to take advantage of opportunities in different tax regimes that apply to buy-and-hold investors on the one hand and to brokers on the other in respect of income and capital gains. Use of insurance via credit default swaps (CDS) and offshore locations for SPVs allowed tax-based returns to financial firms that couldn't be used properly by the investors. This is because the capital gains tax in some jurisdictions is low relative to income tax, and the corporate tax rate is higher. In a sense, by choosing low-quality mortgage-based securities, losses could be optimised to everyone's advantage – provided asset prices stayed firm and a global financial crisis didn't cause liquidity to dry up. As the solvency crisis spread, CDS obligations became one of the key mechanisms for spreading the crisis between banks and insurance companies like AIG.

Why did it happen when it happened?

Many of the trends described so far in this chapter were a fact of financial life for some years, so it's tempting to wonder not only why, but also when, matters came to a head. As we've seen, media coverage often dates the start of the crisis to the tumult of September 2008. But the cracks in the financial system had begun showing well before then: even in early 2007 it was clear that many holders of subprime mortgages would not be able to repay them.

But rather than wonder when exactly the crisis began, it may be more useful to ask when the factors that led to the crisis really started to come together. The answer to that is 2004. As the previous chart shows, that year was marked by something close to an explosion in the issuing of residential mortgage-backed securities – a process that ultimately pumped toxic debt deep into the world's financial system and that governments and banks would struggle to clean up. So, what happened in 2004? The following events were key:

New US policies to encourage home ownership: Enacted the previous year, the Bush Administration's "American Dream" home-owning policies came into force. Their aim was to help poorer Americans afford a down payment on a home. While the policy had good intentions, critics argue that it encouraged many Americans to step on to the property ladder even when there was little hope they could go on making their mortgage payments.

Changes to Fannie Mae and Freddie Mac rules: The United States has a number of "government-sponsored enterprises" designed to ensure the availability of mortgages, especially for poorer families. The two best known are Fannie Mae and Freddie Mac, which buy and securitise mortgages from lenders such as banks, thus freeing banks to provide more home loans. In 2004, the federal government imposed new controls on Fannie Mae and Freddie Mac, which opened the way for banks to move onto their patches. Such a move was probably inevitable: banks and other mortgage firms faced a loss of revenue if they could no longer pass on mortgages to Fannie Mae and Freddie Mac. Their response was to create Fannie and Freddie lookalikes through SIVs, which had the affect of shifting a large quantity of the American mortgage pool from the federal to the private sector.

Publication of Basel II proposals: As discussed above, this effectively encouraged banks to speed up mortgage securitisation.

Changes to rules on investment banks: Finally, 2004 also saw a change in how the Securities and Exchange Commission, or SEC, which regulates the securities business in the United States, supervised investment banks. In return for an agreement from the larger investment banks to let the SEC oversee almost all their activities, the SEC allowed them to greatly reduce their capital requirements, which freed up even more funding to pump into such areas as mortgage securitisation. That move allowed investment banks to go from a theoretical limit of $15 of debt for every dollar in assets to up to $40 for every dollar.

And on to the real world...

What began as a financial crisis quickly morphed into a crisis in the real economy. Beginning in late 2008, global trade began to go into freefall, jobs were lost and economic growth rates plummeted, with countries around the world slumping into recession. In the next chapter we trace how that slowdown spread through the real economy and affected the lives of millions of people around the world.

Find Out More

OECD

On the Internet

To find out about OECD work on financial markets, go to *www.oecd.org/finance*.

Publications

OECD Journal: Financial Market Trends
This twice-yearly periodical provides regular updates on trends and prospects for the international and major domestic financial markets of the OECD area and beyond.

Also of interest

The Current Financial Crisis: Causes and Policy Issues, *OECD Journal: Financial Market Trends*, Blundell-Wignal. A. P. Atkinson and S. Hoon Lee (2009): This paper explores the factors that led up to the crisis, including the emergence of global imbalances and failures in how banks and financial markets were regulated in the years leading up to the crisis.

... AND OTHER SOURCES

Fool's Gold, by Gillian Tett of the *Financial Times*, tells the story of collateralised debt obligations (CDOs) – from their invention at J.P. Morgan in the mid-1990s to their role in causing the crisis. An anthropologist by training, Tett never forgets that it was humans, not financial abstractions, that drove the use – and ultimately misuse – of CDOs.

How Markets Fail, by *The New Yorker*'s John Cassidy, argues that free-market ideology obscured economic realities in recent decades, allowing an unchecked build-up of bubbles in housing and financial markets. The crisis wasn't an accident, says Cassidy, it was inevitable.

Explaining the crisis ... the well-regarded Baseline Scenario blog's "Financial Crisis for Beginners" has original material and links to other useful sources: *http://baselinescenario.com/financial-crisis-for-beginners/*.

As mentioned in Chapter 1, National Public Radio's *This American Life* in the US produced a programme on the causes of the crisis. Go to *www.thisamericanlife.org* and search for episode No. 355, "The Giant Pool of Money", first broadcast on 9 May 2008.

CDOs ... explained in a graphic from *Portfolio* magazine: *www.portfolio.com/interactive-features/2007/12/cdo*

Finance in general ... with just a marker and a whiteboard, Paddy Hirsh of NPR's *Marketplace* explains jargon and the latest developments in finance. *http://marketplace.publicradio.org/collections/coll_display.php?coll_id=20216*

Finance and economics ... regularly discussed in useful background briefings from the independent Council of Foreign Relations in the US: Go to *www.cfr.org* and click on "Backgrounders".

3

The recession had its roots in financial centres like New York and London, but it swiftly spread throughout the global economy. As the scale of the calamity became clear, governments took extraordinary measures to keep financial institutions afloat and stimulate economic demand.

Routes, Reach, Responses

By way of introduction ...

In Dublin, Kelly Lynch is coming to terms with the sudden death of the "Celtic Tiger" – the booming economy that transformed Irish expectations. "Our generation never experienced anything but the Celtic Tiger. We heard about the [recession of the] 1980s, but it was all just whispers and ghost stories. Now it's come back and, yeah, it's a bit of a shock," the 24-year-old told *The Irish Times*.

In Massachusetts, Scott Nicholson is settling in for a morning on his laptop, scouring the Internet for job openings and sending off his CV. Scott, a 24-year-old recent graduate, reckons he applies for four or five jobs a week, but so far he's found only one job, and he rejected that for fear of it becoming a dead end. While confident that his search will eventually pay off, he admits he's surprised at how hard it's been. "I don't think I fully understood the severity of the situation I had graduated into," he told *The New York Times*. His mother, too, is frustrated: "No one on either side of the family has ever gone through this," she said, "and I guess I'm impatient. I know he is educated and has a great work ethic and wants to start contributing, and I don't know what to do."

In Bangkok, Witaya Rakswong is learning to live on less. He used to work as a sous chef in a luxury hotel in Thailand. Then he worked in a bar in Bangkok until its customers stopped coming. Now he's cooking in a cafe on the outskirts of the Thai capital, earning 60% of his hotel salary. "If you spend it wisely, you'd be able to get by," the 37-year-old told World Bank researchers. "Getting by" has meant cutting his mother's allowance by a fifth. "It hurts everybody," he said. "Even if you're not laid off, you're still affected by the crisis, because you're stuck with more work to do for the same or less money. It stresses me out sometimes ...."

Different stories, different continents, but all united by one thing: the recession. After the financial crisis of 2008 came an economic downturn that saw world GDP fall by an estimated 2.1% in 2009 – the first contraction in the global economy since 1945. Even more striking was how it hit so many of the world's economies. While the extent to which economies slowed varied, most suffered some sort of setback, making this truly a global crisis, perhaps the first of its kind.

▶ This chapter looks first at some of the routes the recession took through economies and then at its global reach. The recession may have its roots in the financial centres of developed countries, but its impact stretched far beyond to include emerging and developing countries. Finally, we'll look at how governments moved to tackle the crisis.

What were the routes of recession?

Even in 2007, well before the collapse of Lehman Brothers, the world economy looked to be losing steam. Any slowdown is a matter for concern, but not necessarily of alarm. Recessions, after all, are nothing new, even if their causes vary greatly. Some are due to a shock to the economic system, like the oil crisis of the early 1970s. Others form part of what's called the "business cycle", and can represent a marked but normal cooling in an overheated economy.

What is a recession?	
A **recession** is a period when an economy grows more slowly or shrinks (sometimes called "negative growth"). In technical terms, it's usually defined as two consecutive quarters – that's six months – of economic slowdown or contraction. (In the United States, a wider range of economic indicators, such as unemployment rates, is also considered.) When does a recession become a **depression**? There's no technical definition of this term, but it's generally understood as an unusually severe and long-lasting recession, such as the Great Depression that struck in the 1930s.	

But a slowdown with its roots in a banking crisis is different, and much more worrying. "When Lehman collapsed ... there were tremendous fears about what was going to come next," says Sveinbjörn Blöndal, an economist at the OECD. "Banks play such a central role in our economy. They control the payments system. And you can just imagine what happens when that breaks down."

During such a slowdown, the falloff in economic output tends to be two to three times greater than in a regular downturn, while full recovery can take twice as long. There are several reasons for this. For example, problems in banks may make them less able or less willing to lend. That, in turn, makes borrowing more expensive, which means businesses may put off expansion and consumers postpone big purchases. Also, banking crises tend to be associated with falls in wealth: during this crisis, businesses and consumers saw the value of property and shares tumble. Research in the United States suggests that house prices slide by an average of just over 35% in a financial crisis. Falls like that make consumers less willing to spend and less able to borrow (remortgaging a house that's fallen in value will bring in much less money). A banking crisis can also produce a negative feedback loop – in essence, bad news in the financial sector hits the mood in the "real" economy, which then feeds back into banking and finance.

Let's look now at some of the ways this recession spread through the global economy, first in developed countries and then in emerging and developing economies.

House prices fell: Declining house prices helped trigger the financial crisis in the first place. As the crisis deepened its grip, mortgage markets tightened, meaning home loans became more expensive and harder to obtain, so adding to the initial downturn in prices. House prices have continued to fall in many OECD countries, leading to reduced investment in new construction and so reducing overall economic activity.

Banks got nervous: A key feature of the early stages of the crisis was that banks stopped lending to each other, making it much harder for them to cope with short-term cash-flow problems. This reluctance was hardly surprising: a bank with problem assets on its own books wouldn't need too much imagination to see that other banks, too, might have difficulties. Banks were not alone in finding it hard to borrow. Businesses and consumers were also hit by a "credit crunch" that made loans scarce and more expensive.

Consumers lost confidence: The housing slowdown affected consumers, too. In some countries, especially the United States, consumers tend to spend less as the value of their houses and shareholdings decline. This is not just because they feel less wealthy, and thus a need to be more prudent, but also, as we've seen, because the ability to use their homes as collateral for loans diminishes.

But falling house prices are not the only issue with consumers. Less tangible, but arguably just as important, is consumer confidence. As the state of an economy worsens, people's fears about their own finances grow and they spend less, especially on big-ticket items like cars and televisions. Such cutbacks might not seem like much in the context of the overall economy, but they can quickly add up. If one out of three people planning to replace their cars this year decides to wait until next year, car sales drop by a third. Because consumer confidence has a real impact on how the economy performs, it is regularly measured in specialised surveys that typically ask respondents to rate their own and their country's financial prospects over the next 12 months. As the chart shows, consumer confidence dips as economies slow. During the recession, the fall across the

OECD area was very sharp indeed, and at one stage it stood at its lowest level in more than 30 years.

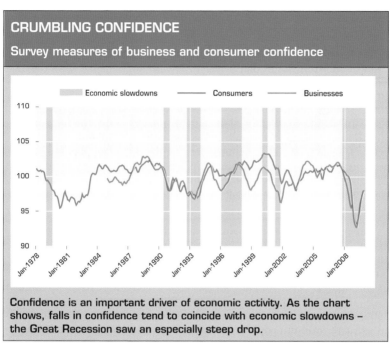

CRUMBLING CONFIDENCE

Survey measures of business and consumer confidence

Confidence is an important driver of economic activity. As the chart shows, falls in confidence tend to coincide with economic slowdowns – the Great Recession saw an especially steep drop.

Source: OECD Factbook 2010.

StatLink ⟨⟨⟨ *http://dx.doi.org/10.1787/888932320561*

Businesses reined back: The credit crunch had a serious impact on businesses, especially smaller and medium-size companies, leading many to become extra cautious and to cancel or delay investment. Businesses also cut back on current spending, as opposed to capital or infrastructure spending: some lowered wages (sometimes in exchange for employment commitments), so reducing workers' spending power, and wherever possible deferred payments, forcing suppliers to go back to banks for expensive short-term loans.

Just as with consumers, confidence is also an issue for businesses, and is closely monitored by officials, through soundings such as the Japanese central bank's closely watched "tankan" survey, and by business itself. One such is an annual global survey of CEOs by business consultants PricewaterhouseCoopers. The 2009 survey was carried out between September and December 2008, a period when the full scale of the financial crisis finally began to hit home. Between the start and the end of the survey period, the number of CEOs who said they were confident about their company's short-term prospects fell from 42% to just 11%. One CEO told the survey, "If I can get three good nights' sleep in the next 12 months, I will consider the year to be a success."

Trade collapsed: It's hard to overstate the speed and scale of the collapse of world trade that began in late 2008. To put it in context, world trade had grown annually by an average of just over 7% in the 10 years up to 2006, hitting 7.3% in 2007. And then the crisis hit: in 2008, growth fell to just 3%, while in 2009 it contracted by about 12%. In itself, that sharp fall was a reflection of the emerging recession; consumer demand collapsed while tightening financial markets made it harder for exporters to get the financing they typically need to bridge the gap between delivery of goods and payment. But the fall also helped drive the recession, helping it to go global and, as we'll see later, delivering it to the doorsteps of emerging and developing economies.

Unemployment rose: Of course, the price of a recession is felt not just in the economy but also in society. Unemployment hit just under 10% in the United States in December 2009 (falling back to 9.7% the following month), which was more than double the 2007 rate of 4.6%. In the euro zone, the figure for December 2009 was 10%, up from 7.5% in 2007. To put those numbers in perspective, even by mid-2009, when unemployment in the OECD area stood at 8.3%, it meant an extra 15 million people were out of work compared with 2007. By the end of 2009, the unemployment rate had risen still further, to 8.8%.

Clearly, unemployment is a reflection of slower economic activity, but by reducing people's spending power and forcing governments to increase social spending it's also a cause. And behind the bald statistics there's the human cost of unemployment, which in extreme cases will force some families below the poverty line. Indeed, as we'll see in the next chapter, it is the most disadvantaged groups of workers – young people, low-skilled, immigrants and temporary workers – who are bearing the brunt of job cuts. These tend also to have relatively limited access to welfare support, and may face serious difficulty in finding a new job, running the risk of their entering the ranks of the long-term unemployed.

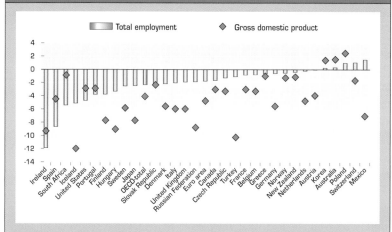

DEPTHS OF THE CRISIS

Falling growth and rising unemployment in the recession

This chart shows the decline in economic output and the rise in unemployment between the first quarter of 2008 and the third quarter of 2009. As the numbers show, very few **OECD** economies avoided a slowdown and even fewer an increase in unemployment. While economic performance has generally recovered, higher rates of joblessness will linger longer.

Source: OECD Factbook 2010.

StatLink ᴹᴼ᙮ᵉ *http://dx.doi.org/10.1787/888932320580*

How far did the recession reach?

If a single word can be used to describe the recession, it might be this: simultaneous. As never before, the economies of the world were struck sharply, suddenly and at the same time, even those a long way removed from the troubled banks and crashing house prices of developed countries. What varied – and varied considerably – was how far they fell and how quickly they recovered.

Emerging economies

At first it appeared that China would suffer very badly during the slowdown. Early in 2009, Chinese officials were reporting that 20 million migrant workers had lost their jobs as demand for goods from customers in the United States and Europe collapsed. But, a year later, Chinese officials were still able to report growth for the year at above 8% – a performance that left China "in extraordinarily better shape than many forecasters had expected", an Asian Development Bank (ADB) report notes.

What happened? China was certainly hit hard by the crisis: as the ADB notes, exports at one stage fell by almost 53% from their pre-crisis levels. But Beijing moved quickly in late 2008 to stimulate the economy through massive state spending, unveiling a package worth 4 trillion yuan, or more than $580 billion. Further stimulus came in the form of a big boost to the money supply and greatly increased lending.

China was not alone. Other major emerging economies, such as Brazil and especially India, weathered the economic storm relatively well – so well, in fact, that they have helped drive recovery in the global economy.

> **"The upturn in the major non-OECD countries, especially in Asia and particularly in China, is now a well established source of strength for the more feeble OECD recovery."**
>
> *OECD Economic Outlook, Vol. 2009/2*

Indeed, the relative strength of some of the "BRIC" (Brazil, Russia, India and China) economies has led some commentators to describe the crisis as a watershed moment. "Their relative rise appears to be stronger despite the rather pitifully thought-out views by some a few months ago that the BRIC 'dream' could be shattered by the crisis," Goldman Sachs economist Jim O'Neill, who famously coined the term BRICs, told Reuters. "We now conceive of China challenging the US for No. 1 slot by 2027 and ... the combined GDP of the four BRICs being potentially bigger than that of the G7 within the next 20 years. This is around 10 years earlier than when we first looked at the issue."

Developing economies

If some of the BRICs can be said to have had a "good" recession, the situation is less clear for developing economies. Even though banks in many of these countries had little or no exposure to the toxic debt of banks in the OECD area, their economies were still hit by the slowdown, although the extent to which this happened varied greatly.

For example, the developing countries of Europe and Central Asia were particularly hard hit, in part because of problems that existed even before the crisis. According to the World Bank, the region's GDP fell by more than 6% in 2009, and looks set for only a very feeble recovery.

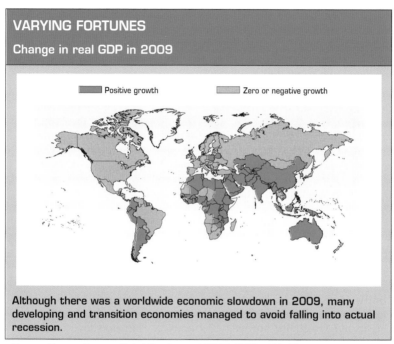

VARYING FORTUNES

Change in real GDP in 2009

Although there was a worldwide economic slowdown in 2009, many developing and transition economies managed to avoid falling into actual recession.

Source: *Perspectives on Global Development 2010: Shifting Wealth.*

StatLink ᴀᴵˢᴸ *http://dx.doi.org/10.1787/888932320599*

Much of Africa managed to avoid falling into actual recession: according to the African Development Bank only six countries saw a contraction in GDP in 2009. However, many more saw growth rates slow, putting at risk some of the progress African countries have made in recent years, especially in sub-Saharan Africa. According to AfDB economists, GDP overall in Africa probably grew by only 2% in 2009, a sharp decline on the annual pace of 6% seen in the seven or eight years before the crisis. The AfDB also forecast that during 2009, the continent would see its first decline in real GDP per capita in almost a decade.

The crisis made its way to developing countries through a number of routes. For example, as the crisis began to bite in late 2008, prices fell sharply for such commodities as food, metals and minerals (although there was a recovery in 2009). Emerging and developing countries were also hit by the wider slowdown in global trade, especially a slowdown in imports to OECD countries as consumers in the zone tightened their belts and businesses reduced output. As financial markets froze up, importers and exporters also found it increasingly hard to access various forms of trade credit, which, in simple terms, is credit to bridge the gap between when goods are delivered and when they're paid for.

Developing economies also saw a substantial drop in financial flows from abroad. The World Bank estimates that FDI – foreign direct investment – in 2009 stood at $385 billion, just 30% of levels in the previous year. Foreign aid has also been hit as governments in developed countries come under pressure to sort out their own countries' problems. Although it's forecast to reach record levels in 2010 in dollar terms, official development assistance will be well down from what developing countries were expecting. For example, commitments given at the G8's Gleneagles summit in 2005 mean African countries should have received aid worth $25 billion in 2010; in reality, they'll probably get only about $12 billion.

And developing countries were hit by a drop in remittances, the money sent back home by emigrants. This can play an important role in easing poverty in some of the world's poorest countries, allowing families to eat better, build homes and even start small businesses. During previous recessions, remittances have sometimes remained surprisingly resilient; however, the scale of this slowdown and the fact that it has affected so many of the world's economies means they have come under pressure. According to the World Bank, recorded remittances to developing countries were worth $388 billion in 2008, a new record that continued the strong growth seen in recent years. In 2009, however, they are estimated to have fallen by 6.1% and look unlikely to return to 2008 levels even by 2011.

Policy responses	

The scale of the potential problems facing developing countries was recognised by the international community. For instance, at their summit in London in April 2009, leaders of the G20 countries agreed to treble resources available to the International Monetary Fund to support developing economies in trouble. Despite such responses, and repeated promises by donor governments to meet their aid commitments, there is clear concern that development aid could fall as governments in developed countries seek to fix their own economies and cut back on spending. Any such cutbacks could represent a major blow to already hard-hit developing countries.

Life and death impact

Through joblessness and reduced income, the recession will damage the lives of many people in developed countries. In developing countries, however, it is literally a matter of life and death. According to World Bank estimates, an extra 30 000 to 40 000 children will have died in Sub-Saharan Africa in 2009 as a result of the slowdown in economic growth and the subsequent increase in poverty. And by the end of 2010, the bank estimates an additional 64 million people in some of the world's poorest countries will be living in extreme poverty due to factors like falling remittances and rising unemployment, especially in sectors that rely heavily on exports.

For example, Cambodia's garment industry – which accounts for about 70% of the country's exports – laid off about one in six workers in the first half of 2009 as collapsing US demand pushed exports down by about 30%. Most of these workers are women, and the loss of their jobs can have a big impact on their families. "My family's living conditions are very difficult now because they depend on me and the money I've been sending home," Sophorn, an unemployed textile worker, told a reporter in Phnom Penh. "Seven people are dependent on me." Workers forced out of their jobs may have little choice but to return to farming for their livelihoods, which can mean a large cut in family incomes. In turn, that may mean their children are deprived of decent nutrition and education, which not only threatens their short-term survival but also risks having a long-term impact both on their individual development and on national social and economic progress.

How did governments respond?

The scale of the financial crisis and recession spurred swift government responses. As we saw earlier, because the slowdown had its roots in a banking crisis, governments had reason to be especially concerned. Equally, the fact that it struck so much of the global economy simultaneously put a fresh emphasis on the need for countries to work together. To conclude this chapter, we'll look briefly at the responses of governments and central banks to the crisis, which can be examined under three main headings: support for banks and financial markets, monetary policy and fiscal policy.

Supporting banks

Money is sometimes described as the lifeblood of the economy; if that's the case, financial markets – for all the problems they have created – are like the heart. If markets are not functioning well, the processes that are essential to modern economies – borrowing, lending, raising funds and so on – risk grinding to a halt. Indeed, to some extent, that happened during the crisis, with crushing consequences for the wider economy.

Three main problems plagued banks and financial institutions:

➤ **A breakdown of trust**: Doubts about the scale of toxic assets on bank books and about financial institutions' potential future liabilities ate away at trust in financial markets, seizing up normal lending and borrowing.

➤ **Under-capitalisation**: As we saw in the previous chapter, in the run-up to the crisis banks found ways to lend more and more money without a corresponding increase in their capital base. However, major losses in mortgage lending left big holes in banks' balance sheets, leaving them badly in need of capital. But that proved difficult to find.

➤ **Weak liquidity**: For banks, liquidity essentially means having sufficient funds to meet their obligations, for instance, when customers seek to withdraw money from their accounts. At its worst, insufficient liquidity can end in a run, where a bank is unable to pay money it owes to panicking depositors.

Although substantial problems remain among some banks and other financial institutions, the rapid response of governments averted what some feared would become a meltdown in global financial markets. Action included huge injections of capital into banks, bank nationalisations, increases in insurance on bank deposits and steps to guarantee or purchase bank debts. The price of this support has been staggering. According to OECD estimates, governments have made commitments worth a total of $11.4 trillion – equivalent to the 2007 GDP of Japan, the United Kingdom, Germany and France combined or, put another way, $1 600 for every man, woman and child on the planet. (Note, these are worst-case scenario commitments, not actual spending to support the banks.)

Much government action has focused on "insulating" banks from their troubled assets: as long as these remained on banks' books, they undermined confidence and trust in financial markets. Since the crisis began, a number of approaches have emerged:

> **Ring-fencing:** The first involves ring-fencing bad assets – governments provide guarantees for the value of such assets, which are removed from the bank's balance sheets and managed separately, allowing the bank to resume normal lending. This process was carried out on a substantial scale in the United States and the United Kingdom. For example, assets guaranteed at Lloyds TSB and the Royal Bank of Scotland at one stage amounted to 38% of UK GDP.

> **The "bad bank":** A more systematic approach is the creation of a bad bank – effectively, a centralised asset-management company that buys troubled assets from banks, which should leave them free to resume normal lending. In Ireland, the government has set up a bad bank called the National Asset Management Agency (NAMA) to buy troubled loans from banks, especially those made to developers whose empires fell apart as property prices collapsed. However, with the market locked in the doldrums, there's been intense debate over how much NAMA should pay for such assets. A shortage of sales means the market is not sending clear signals of what it thinks property is worth.

> **Nationalisation:** As a last resort, banks were nationalised in some countries, although that still leaves governments facing the problem of how to deal with bad assets.

Actions such as these did much to safeguard the banking sector, but challenges remain. For instance, in Europe there's concern about the scale of banks' holdings of government bonds issued by some eurozone economies. As we'll see later, markets have become "jittery" about the capacity of some governments to honour their bonds. In turn, that can affect existing holders of such bonds, such as banks, making it more expensive for them to borrow and, thus, less willing to lend.

Longer term, governments will also need to find ways to safely reverse the steps they took, for example selling off the bank assets they've taken on. This will need to be done slowly to avoid flooding the market. And as we'll see in Chapter 6, there will also need to be a thorough rethink of financial regulation, although governments differ on when this should be done. Quite simply, current regulations failed. They led to – and even encouraged – dangerous practices in the financial sector, such as a lack of transparency, the creation of bank compensation packages that rewarded reckless behaviour, a misguided reliance on ratings and illusory financial models, and an overall financial system that was "pro-cyclical" – it pumped extra heat into a warming economy and poured on cold water when it began to cool.

Monetary policy

When economies slow, central banks usually try to push down interest rates. The logic of this is that if rates are low, businesses and consumers will be more likely to borrow and thus to spend or invest those borrowings, so generating economic activity. By contrast, raising interest rates can help to cool down an overheating economy by making borrowing more expensive.

What are fiscal and monetary policies?	
The two great weapons typically used to fight downturns, and even to steer economies through good times, are fiscal and monetary policy. In basic terms, **fiscal policy** refers to government spending and tax collection. Of course, governments affect economies in other ways, too, such as the ways in which they design competition and education policy, but these are longer-term issues and less related to the immediate task of tackling a recession. **Monetary policy** is usually set by central banks, which in many countries are independent of government, and largely relates to setting interest rates and controlling liquidity.	

Central banks don't directly set rates on the sort of loans that most of us take out from regular banks. Instead, they set a short-term or overnight rate at which they lend to other banks, and this in turn influences rates set by other financial institutions. Typically, a central bank sets a target for this overnight rate, which is known as its **key interest rate** or **policy rate**. The sharpness of the slowdown led to unprecedented cuts in policy rates across the OECD area: in the United States, Japan and the United Kingdom, rates stood at between 0% and 0.25% in early 2010, and at 1.0% in the euro zone – extremely low by historical standards.

Setting interest rates is a key weapon in the economic armoury, but there is an obvious limit to what can be done: once rates hit 0%, they can't really go any lower (although Sweden has experimented with subzero rates). For that reason, some central banks pursued other ways to support and kick-start the financial system, falling back on such unconventional monetary policy measures as liquidity injections and purchasing financial assets. In simple terms, the latter can involve a central bank buying government bonds from banks, which increases the banks' stock of cash, which can then be lent to businesses and consumers, so stimulating economic activity.

Because central banks have effectively pumped more liquidity into the financial system, some observers have warned that this could fuel **inflation** (which can be thought of in the sense of a single unit of currency – a dollar, a yen, a euro – no longer being able to buy as much as it used to). These fears are probably overstated: high unemployment and what economists refer to as "low capacity utilisation" – workers who aren't working or plants that are shuttered or not operating at their full capacity – should limit inflationary price rises. As economies recover over the longer term, however, loose monetary policies will need to be tightened to keep inflation at bay.

Fiscal policy

Government debt *(see box)* tends to rise during a recession. Forecasts for this slowdown suggest gross government debt in the OECD area will rise by about 30 percentage points to more than 100% of GDP in 2011. There are two main reasons for this. First, during a slump, governments earn less from tax – for example, rising unemployment means fewer people pay income tax and falling profits mean companies pay lower corporate taxes. Second, because of the existence of the social safety net, there is an automatic increase in government spending on things like unemployment benefits as more people lose their jobs. These changes are referred to by economists as "automatic stabilisers": in other words, they tend to cool down economies when they're heating up (by taking money out of the economy), and to support economies when they're cooling down (by pumping money back in). In theory, automatic stabilizers are just that – automatic: they shouldn't require special intervention by governments to begin operating.

What are government debts and deficits?

A **government deficit** (also known as a "budget deficit" or "fiscal deficit") is created when a government spends more in a year than it earns. Deficits have risen during the crisis, and are projected to be equivalent to 8.25% of GDP in 2010 across the OECD area, the highest level for many decades. **Government debt** (sometimes called the "national debt" or "public debt") represents a government's accumulated deficits plus other off-budget items – in effect, borrowings built up year after year. For 2011, government debt across the OECD area is forecast to exceed total GDP, an increase of about 30 percentage points since before the crisis. In other words, governments will owe more than their countries' entire annual economic output.

But during a recession governments may also decide to take special – or "discretionary" – action, which is something virtually every OECD country did, although the size and scope of these packages varied greatly. In the United States, for instance, the size of the fiscal package was equivalent to 5.5% of 2008's GDP. And in Australia, Canada, Korea and New Zealand it was worth at least 4%. By contrast, in a few countries (particularly Hungary, Iceland and Ireland), the weak state of government finances means they have had to tighten up their fiscal position, through actions such as reducing spending and raising taxation.

What did governments do? Tax cuts have formed a big part of the mix, in particular reducing income taxes. The logic of this is simple: spending on infrastructure like new roads, for example, takes time to design and implement (think of how long it might take to draw up plans, win planning approval and issue building contracts); by contrast, changes in tax codes can be announced and implemented almost overnight. That said, countries also increased public investment, which includes providing extra money for things like education and infrastructure, and gave special support to industries such as car-making. Governments also sought to boost consumer spending with programmes such as car "scrappage" schemes (nicknamed "cash for clunkers" in the US), which typically gave motorists a trade-in on their old cars of between $1 500 and $2 000.

The multiplier effect

What's the impact of such packages? It can turn out to be greater than the headline numbers might suggest, thanks to a phenomenon called the "multiplier effect". In simple terms, this means that for every dollar the government spends, the total economic impact may be worth more than a dollar: for example, if a government pumps extra money into, say, healthcare, that may mean extra income for doctors and nurses or suppliers, who in turn may spend some of this money on home improvements, which means extra income for builders, and so on. (And that doesn't include the social benefits that may result from extra health spending.) In theory, this could go on forever; in practice, it doesn't. Some of the money will be spent on imports, meaning the benefits leak into other economies. Also, increased government spending may lead people to save more and spend less as they face up to the prospect of higher taxes in the future to pay for all that government spending.

Measuring the multiplier effect is hard at the best of times, but in a recession it's especially difficult. For example, the heightened sense of economic uncertainty may lead people to save even more than they normally would, so reducing the benefits. There are also variations between the multiplier effect of spending and revenue measures: for example, governments may be able to target infrastructure investment in ways that maximise the knock-on benefits; by contrast, cuts in personal income tax may have fewer benefits, simply because people choose to save the extra money. Finally, the size and nature of an economy can also play a role in determining the scale of the effect: in small, open economies more of the additional income generated by the multiplier effect is likely to leak out through spending on imports, so reducing the overall impact.

Paying the price ...

By the end of 2009, almost every OECD country had emerged from recession, although their recoveries were modest and there was little expectation of a strong growth in the immediate future. And even as growth rates recovered, unemployment remained stubbornly high.

This uncertain background meant governments faced a big challenge in implementing "exit strategies" – in other words, timing the withdrawal of special support measures for banks and the wider economy. On the one hand, they wanted to ensure they didn't move too quickly and choke off any faltering recovery; on the other, they knew that deficits couldn't be allowed to go on rising indefinitely. For some economies, especially some on the periphery of the euro zone, such as Greece, concern over rising deficits became acute in the wake of the crisis. That made it increasingly expensive for them to borrow on international markets and meant tough action to get their public finances under control.

They were not alone, even if their problems were more severe than others'. As we'll see in Chapter 7, sooner or later governments in many OECD countries will need to take tough decisions on reducing budget deficits, probably through a mix of lower spending and higher taxes, meaning that we're all going to be paying the price of this recession for years to come. Before then, let's look in the next chapter at how increasing numbers of people are already paying a price through unemployment.

Find Out More

OECD

On the Internet

For an introduction to OECD work on **economics**, go to *www.oecd.org/economics*.

For the latest **economic data** from the OECD, go to *www.oecd.org/std/mei* or key in "OECD key tables" to a search engine. For the latest update on the OECD's **leading indicators**, which are designed to provide early signals of turning points in economic activity, go to *www.oecd.org/std/cli*.

For the latest from the OECD on the **recession and recovery**, go to *www.oecd.org* and click on the "From Crisis to Recovery" logo.

For analysis and insights on the state of Africa's economies from the OECD's Development Centre, go to *www.africaneconomicoutlook.org*.

Publications

OECD Economic Outlook: Published twice yearly, the *OECD Economic Outlook* analyses the major trends and forces shaping short-term economic prospects. It also provides in-depth coverage of the economic policy measures required to foster growth and stable prices in OECD and other major economies.

Going for Growth: Published annually, *Going for Growth* provides an overview of structural policy developments in OECD countries. The series uses a broad set of indicators of structural policies and performance to suggest policy reforms for each country with the aim of raising labour productivity and utilisation. It provides internationally comparable indicators that enable countries to assess their economic performance and structural policies in a broad range of areas.

OECD Economic surveys: An economic survey is published every 18 months to two years for each OECD country. In addition, regular economic assessments are produced for a number of other countries, including Brazil, China, India and Russia. To find out more go to *www.oecd.org/eco/surveys*.

... AND OTHER SOURCES

World Bank and IMF: Both the World Bank and International Monetary Fund have created special sections on their websites focusing on the recession and recovery: go to *www.worldbank.org/financialcrisis* and *www.imf.org/external/np/exr/key/finstab.htm*.

Regional development banks: The latest state of Asia's economies is examined in the Asian Development Bank's *Asian Development Outlook* (*www.adb.org/Documents/Books/ADO*); coverage of Latin America and South America can be found on the website of the Inter-American Development Bank (*www.iadb.org*); for Africa, go to the African Development Bank's site (*www.afdb.org*); for Central Europe and Central Asia, go to the site of the European Bank for Reconstruction and Development (*www.ebrd.org*).

National economic research organisations: Many countries have institutions that carry out research into how national economies work and the interaction between economic and social forces. For a list of such bodies, go to *www.oecd.org/economics* and click on "NERO Homepage".

4

When the crisis struck, employment in OECD countries was at its highest level since 1980, but the first victims of unemployment were the same groups as in previous decades such as the young and temporary workers. Employment takes longer to recover than output, and governments can play a role in helping those worst affected.

The Impacts
on Jobs

By way of introduction...

Being forced out of a job is an unpleasant experience. Employers often prefer to use euphemisms such as "I'll have to let you go" that imply it's somehow liberating or what the worker wanted. Thomas Carlyle, the man who coined the expression "the dismal science" to describe economics, was much nearer the mark. Writing in 1840, he claimed that "A man willing to work, and unable to find work, is perhaps the saddest sight that fortune's inequality exhibits under this sun."

Modern research supports Carlyle's view. For instance, finding yourself unemployed has a more detrimental effect on mental health than other life changes, including losing a partner or being involved in an accident. A long spell of joblessness has social costs too, whether at the level of individuals and families or whole communities.

▶ Tackling unemployment and its consequences has to be a major part of governments' response to the crisis. This chapter looks at the workers and sectors most affected by the crisis and how policies can help workers weather the storm.

Which jobs are affected?

In most respects, the present crisis is like previous ones in the way it affects different sectors of the economy and categories of workers, even though the speed and scale of the changes are different. Typically, construction is the first industry to be hit during a downturn. Historical data show that labour demand in this sector is 70% more sensitive to the highs and lows of the business cycle than the average across all sectors. Today's crisis actually started in the subprime mortgage market, and even if it had gone no further, US construction workers and firms would have suffered from the drop in demand as financing for new homes dried up. Elsewhere, the bursting of property bubbles had immediate, dramatic effects. Ireland and Spain were hit particularly hard, with employment in construction down by 37% and 25%, respectively, over the twelve months ending in the second quarter of 2009.

Historical patterns suggest that after construction, durable goods would be the hardest hit. While less volatile than construction, this sector has still been 40% more sensitive to the business cycle than the average. The difficulties of the auto industry show how the financial crisis soon spread to the "real" economy. Given the global nature of the durable goods sector, the unprecedented downturn in world trade (over 10% in 2009) greatly aggravated the employment situation to the point where employment losses in this sector have been steeper than those in construction in many OECD countries.

We tend to associate the auto industry with the countries that the big car makers are based in, and most of the jobs lost have been in these countries. But looking at a smaller country with no domestic producer is revealing about the concrete reality of many of the things we talk about in this book, such as the importance of trade linkages. Five thousand New Zealand workers lost jobs in the car industry in the six months to April 2009. That's a tenth of the people involved in importing and selling cars. As the *National Business Review* points out, imports were supporting a range of jobs such as cafeteria workers in the ports, and not just the obvious ones in dealerships or auto financing companies.

Surprisingly, in view of the origins of the crisis, the impact on employment in the US financial services sector is not as bad as you might expect, despite spectacular job losses in some of the big banks and other financial institutions. Across the sector, employment losses were 6.9%, compared with 5% in the economy as a whole. Although financial and other business services are feeling the impact of the recession hitting their clients, employment has held up much better in the overall services sector (-2.9%) than in the goods producing sector (-17%). Nonetheless, the much larger services sector accounts for nearly half (46%) of the total decline in employment.

Some sectors are relatively insensitive to cyclical effects, in part due to the nature of their business. Agriculture is the least affected, because it is not possible to simply halt most production and wait for things to get better, and agricultural employment is low in most OECD countries anyway. Utilities such as water and electricity continue to be in demand, even if, like agriculture, a poorer economic climate does eventually reduce demand from some customers.

Which workers are most affected?

The crisis affects different sectors in different ways, but the impact also varies according to age, gender, skill level and type of contract. Once again, layoffs are following patterns seen before and are similar to what you might expect, at least in most instances.

The cost to employers of hiring and firing workers (turnover costs) is important here. Turnover costs for young people are lower than for others, since they have relatively little experience and do not benefit much from any seniority rules. Over the past 15 years or so, the youth unemployment rate has been over 2.5 times higher than that of workers aged 25 to 54 ("prime age" workers) in OECD countries. Sensitivity to business cycles is twice as high for younger workers as for those of prime age, and 70% to 80% above the national average. Older workers are about 20% more sensitive to business cycles than prime age workers, but no more sensitive than the national average. We'll look at how the crisis affects the employment of young people in more detail below.

Workers on temporary contracts are also more likely to lose their job than permanent workers. During the current economic downturn, 85% of job losses in Spain concerned temporary workers. In Italy the figure for net job losses (not including the self-employed, who were also affected) can be explained by the drop in the number of temporary jobs, since for permanent jobs, figures for hiring and firing were about the same.

Higher skill levels tend to lessen the chances of being unemployed, partly because workers may move to a lower skilled occupation, and partly because firms wait longer before laying off a skilled worker who will be more difficult to replace when business picks up.

Looking at the data from past and the present downturns in the business cycle does, however, throw up surprises. First, gender has not made any difference to the chances of losing your job in past recessions. However, this may be due to the fact that construction and other hard-hit occupations are male-dominated. Looking at women and men in the same line of work substantially increases the relative volatility of female employment.

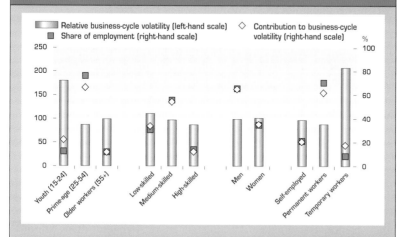

BUSINESS-CYCLE SENSITIVITY OF DIFFERENT GROUPS OF WORKERS

National average = 100

Age and type of contract have the biggest influence on the likelihood of being affected by a recession. Young workers and those on temporary contracts are the most vulnerable. And young workers on temporary contracts are doubly vulnerable

Source: OECD Employment Outlook 2009.

StatLink *http://dx.doi.org/10.1787/888932320618*

That said, the current crisis has actually hit men harder than women. On average for OECD Europe, male employment dropped by 2.9% in the year to the second quarter of 2009, whereas the figure was only 0.3% for women. The greater-than-typical concentration of job losses in construction and manufacturing, which is associated with the bursting of the housing price bubble and unprecedented decline in international trade flows, explains why men are bearing the brunt of rising unemployment.

Youth: a lost generation?

Before the crisis, the youth unemployment rate declined slightly, from 15% in the mid-1990s to 13% in the mid-2000s, although, as mentioned above, young people were still more than 2.5 times as likely to be unemployed than others. There were also big differences from one country to another. In Germany the ratio of youth to adult unemployment was 1.5, largely because of an apprenticeship system that ensures a smooth transition from school to work for most people. The ratio was close to 3 in some of the Continental and Southern European countries, where about one in five youth in the labour market was unemployed. In Sweden, where the "last-in first-out" rule is strictly enforced in the case of layoffs, the ratio was above four. A number of factors help to explain why youth employment is more sensitive to the business cycle. The main ones are the high share of young people in temporary jobs and their disproportionate concentration in certain cyclically sensitive industries.

Coping with a job loss in a recession and the likely protracted period of unemployment is difficult for anyone, but for disadvantaged youth lacking basic education, failure to find a first job or keep it for long can have long-term consequences that some experts refer to as "scarring". Scarring means that the simple fact of being unemployed increases the risk that it will happen again or that future earnings will be reduced, mainly through a deterioration of skills and missing work experience, or because potential employers think the person concerned was unemployed because he or she is less productive than other candidates. Income is affected more strongly than future employment prospects, and in particular by unemployment immediately upon graduation from college.

Beyond the effects on wages and employability, spells of unemployment while young often create permanent scars through the harmful effects on a number of other outcomes many years later, including happiness, job satisfaction and health. Moreover, spells of unemployment tend to be particularly harmful to the individual – and to society – when the most disadvantaged youth become unemployed.

A "mutual obligations" approach sometimes works well for disadvantaged youth. In exchange for income support, jobseekers need to participate in training, job-search or job-placement activities. That said, governments should not underestimate the difficulties of implementing a labour market policy based on acquiring skills first, working later. The international evidence from evaluations of training programmes for disadvantaged youth is not very encouraging, and when unemployment levels rise suddenly, it may be difficult to meet both quantity and quality objectives for training programmes.

The experience of Japan during the so-called "lost decade" of the 1990s is instructive about the long-lasting effects for the generation of youth entering the labour market during the crisis. Not only were youth disproportionally affected by unemployment during the lost decade, but many had to accept non-regular (temporary and part-time) jobs even when the economy finally recovered in the early 2000s. Many employers preferred to hire "fresh" graduates for career-track jobs, leaving victims of the crisis trapped in long-term unemployment or repeated periods of inactivity.

School-to-work programmes could help the current generation of school-leavers to get off to a good start. For example, the United Kingdom implemented measures in order to "not write off a generation of young people, or allow their talents to be wasted" by losing touch with the labour market. However, young people who have become discouraged by lack of success in finding a job may become sceptical about jobs initiatives, and these programmes should not assume that providing a service is enough. They have to make an effort to go out and contact those they are supposed to help.

One way to do this is to promote early interventions when disadvantaged youth are still in school to make sure that support is available to help them in the transition to work. This is likely to be more successful than trying to persuade people who haven't done well at school to go back to the classroom to upgrade their education and skills after they've left.

Apprenticeships could also help. In a downturn however, employers are more reluctant to offer places, and some apprentices lose their job before completing training. Governments could provide subsidies to promote apprenticeship for unskilled young people and support measures to help apprentices made redundant to complete their training, as France and Australia have done.

Poverty is another threat for young people. Many of the jobs young people take do not qualify for unemployment benefits and are the first to go during a downturn (including temporary, seasonal and interim jobs). More than half of OECD countries have already moved to increase the income of job losers by increasing the unemployment benefits or extending coverage. One way of doing this could be to include internships and work placements in the number of months that count for eligibility.

More generally, the economic downturn might also be an opportunity to reconsider factors that tend to penalise youth even when things are going well. Many employers are reluctant to employ low-skilled youth, because they are just as expensive as more experienced workers. Almost half of the OECD countries with a statutory minimum wage (10 out of 21) have an age-related sub-minimum wage to facilitate access of low-skilled youth to employment. Others have reduced significantly the social security contributions paid by employers for low-paid workers. Another option would be to promote more apprenticeship contracts for low-skilled youth, as the apprenticeship wage is lower than the minimum wage because it implies a training commitment for the employer.

Migrants: particularly vulnerable

Immigrants were already more vulnerable to unemployment than the rest of the population before the recession in most OECD countries, with the notable exception of the United States. In 2006, the unemployment rate of immigrants was twice that of the native-born in Switzerland, in the Netherlands, in Belgium, in Austria and in most Nordic countries.

Migrant workers are particularly vulnerable during a crisis for three reasons. First, they often work in the industries that are most affected by downturns (and upswings) such as construction. Second, turnover costs are often considerably lower for foreign-born workers because they are more likely to be on temporary contracts and have been in the job for a shorter time. Third, they may be victims of discrimination when, amid public concern about the future and the risk to livelihoods, latent resentment of the outsider often crystallises into calls to "stop them stealing our jobs".

The influence of a fourth characteristic is more ambiguous. Immigrants are more likely to be self-employed in many European countries, as well as to some extent in the United States. This could be thanks to their integration in the host country, entrepreneurial talent and desire for independence, but it could also be a last resort in the face of difficulties in finding salaried employment. Businesses owned by immigrants may be more at risk of bankruptcy in the current situation due to the fact that they tend to be smaller; such businesses are often in sectors that the crisis hits first; and they may be geared towards immigrant communities, so the higher risk of unemployment among their clients will have knock-on effects.

Even if there may be a delay before changes in labour migration trends are perceptible, declines are clear already in a number of countries, especially those, such as Ireland and the United Kingdom, where the recession hit first. In the United States, there was a 16% fall in the number of work-related temporary visas (the H-1B visa) between 2008 and the previous year.

It's important to note that not all forms of immigration, and not every country, will be affected equally by the crisis. For a start, not all migration is "discretionary", meaning that the government can stop it at will. Governments are bound by international agreements to allow some kinds of immigration, such as the free movement of workers in the EU or family reunification. In 2006, discretionary labour migration was less than 20% of total flows in most OECD countries and no more than a third of all flows in the leading countries. Family immigration accounts for a large part of immigration into the OECD area, and tends to fall less in response to slowdowns than labour migration.

Declining job opportunities are likely to keep some would-be migrants at home, and governments are also making it harder for immigrants to enter. For example, some countries have reduced the number of permits they issue for temporary labour immigrants. In Spain, the number of non-seasonal workers to be recruited anonymously from abroad (*contingente*) went from 15 731 in 2008 to just 901 in 2009. Italy has also lowered its quota for non-seasonal workers, from 150 000 in 2008 to zero in 2009 (although the quota for seasonal workers has remained unchanged). The UK announced a 5% cut in the number of highly-skilled migrants it would allow to enter the country.

However, countries that traditionally encourage permanent immigration, such as Canada and New Zealand, have made no change to their target levels for new immigrants. Only Australia has reduced the intake in its permanent highly skilled migration programme, by 20% in 2009.

Among other changes are reductions in occupational shortage lists – listings of occupations where workers are in short supply that some countries use in selecting immigrants. There are also signs that countries are reinforcing labour market tests, widely used in the OECD area to determine that no local worker is available to fill a position.

The rationale for such moves is clear. As unemployment rises, there is often a strong temptation to try to reduce the size of the workforce. For example, during the recessions of the 1970s, many European countries shut their doors to the "guest workers" who had been brought in from abroad to help rebuild broken economies after World War II. Rising unemployment also breeds resentment of immigrants, and governments may face calls to preserve "jobs for locals".

But – recession or not – there will remain a long-term need for labour immigration in many countries. The average age of people in OECD countries is rising, sometimes quite rapidly, meaning that in the years to come there will be more retirees depending on fewer active workers. Immigrants will help bridge some – if not all – of this gap. Also, immigrants are key employees in a number of sectors, such as health care. It's unrealistic to believe that workers laid off in other industries can be easily retrained to take their places. Many governments will thus face a challenge to design policies that may reduce migration flows in the short term while taking account of long-term needs.

Are some countries worse off than others?

The downturn hit the United States earlier than most countries. Since the start of the recession in December 2007, the number of unemployed persons grew by 7.9 million, and the unemployment rate doubled, rising from 5.0% to a peak of 10.1% in October 2009. However, unemployment declined slightly between October 2009 and May 2010, suggesting that labour market conditions had stabilised, but that little progress had been made in getting the jobless back to work.

In the euro area, unemployment rose to 10.1% in April 2010 from 7.3% in December 2007. The rise in unemployment in Ireland and Spain was significantly larger, with a sharp fall in house building leading to major job losses in the various jobs that make up the sector. In Ireland, the unemployment rate rose from 4.8% to 13.2%, and in Spain from 8.8% to 19.7%. By contrast, the rise in unemployment has been much smaller in other OECD countries, both in Europe and elsewhere. For example, German unemployment was actually a little lower in April 2010 than in December 2007 (although it did rise slightly in the year up to October 2009, after German exports dropped sharply), while unemployment increased from 3.7% to 5.1% in Japan.

Some of the cross-country differences in how sharply unemployment rose are easily explained by differences in the overall severity of the recession. However, it is surprising that unemployment has not increased much in several countries, including Germany, where the hit to GDP was relatively big.

We talked above about the vulnerability of workers on temporary contracts. In developing countries, this is made even worse by the fact that many workers have no contract at all, beyond a verbal agreement. Up to 60% of the labour force in some developing countries work informally. In India, for example, the official unemployment rate was 4.7% in 2005, but 83% of non-agricultural workers were informal, with jobs but without employment protection, unemployment insurance or pension entitlement. The crisis is likely to lead to a surge in informal employment due to job losses in the formal sector, resulting in deteriorating working conditions and lower wages for the poorest.

Were OECD economies better prepared for this downturn?

The OECD area entered the crisis with the lowest unemployment rate since 1980 and the highest share of the working-age population in a job. This is due in part to more than a decade of "structural" labour market reform, including measures to deter the unemployed from staying on benefit and encourage them to look for work, for instance making payments dependent on actively seeking a job, and a weakening of job protection to make it easier for employers to hire and fire.

These structural reforms have certainly contributed to an improved situation over the long term, but in a crisis, there may be tradeoffs between policies best suited to protect workers' jobs and incomes in the short run, and policies designed to shorten the length of the downturn. For example, stronger employment protection may reduce the immediate increase in unemployment, but if it makes employers wary of hiring, it could cause the extra unemployment that nonetheless results to persist longer. It is likely that past structural reforms will help economies to recover more quickly and prevent unemployment staying at a high level for long. However, it is also likely that some of those same reforms may have caused more workers to lose their jobs during the recession than would otherwise have been the case.

The changes discussed above also suggest a mixed picture regarding workers' capacity to cope with a spell of unemployment, depending on how they are affected by social and economic trends. The expansion in employment before the crisis meant that there was more than one adult working in two-thirds of OECD households before the crisis struck, but many of the "second" wage earners may be in vulnerable jobs such as temporary or part-time work and have little or no right to unemployment benefits. At the same time, the number of one-adult households has grown, and if the adult loses his or her job, the household may have no source of revenue other than welfare benefits. Once again, there are advantages and disadvantages to the changes of recent years, but no strong proof that they have made workers better (or less) able to cope with the recession.

What can government do to help the unemployed?

One thing to remember is that even during a recession, firms hire workers. In February 2009, as the full force of the crisis was being felt, around 4.8 million workers in the United States separated from their jobs (nearly 4% of workers). In the same month, 4.3 million were hired. More workers leaving than starting jobs meant that total employment fell, but the impression you sometimes get that there are only layoffs and no hope for anybody is misleading. In most OECD countries, you could probably find reports of firms having trouble filling vacancies.

However, the reduced number of vacancies means competition for jobs is fierce in a deep recession. For example, the US labour market went from a pre-crisis ratio of 1.5 job seekers for each job opening to more than 6 unemployed competing for each vacancy by the end of 2009. Some categories of workers may be locked out of the labour market because they don't have the skills requested, or even the contacts needed to know about the openings in the first place. In some countries, unemployment rates never recovered after a severe recession. Finland, for example, never got back to the low levels of the 1980s after a recession in the early 1990s.

OECD countries already had a range of programmes in place to help the unemployed when the crisis struck. However, these programmes were designed for much lower levels of unemployment than we see now in many countries, and were intended to get people back to work quickly. Apart from cash benefits for the unemployed, the programmes usually offer help in finding a job, or in finding a training course to improve or acquire skills. As the number of unemployed has soared in many countries, the resources available per unemployed person have fallen. Most of the stimulus packages put in place to respond to the crisis contain extra funding for labour market programmes, but these supplementary funds are small relative to the increase in unemployment in most cases. A few countries, notably Denmark and Switzerland, automatically expand funding for re-employment assistance when unemployment rises, reducing the danger that job losers drift into long-term unemployment or totally disengage from the labour market.

Even with the extra funds, there is the problem of finding qualified staff to implement the programmes. Helping job seekers is a skilled task, and the counsellors and trainers may not be available in sufficient numbers. Some countries are collaborating with private sector agencies to expand re-employment assistance for the unemployed. Presumably, these firms have staff with less to do at a time of reduced labour demand, but they would have to be controlled to make sure they weren't creaming off the most employable workers for their private contracts and extending the length of time the others were unemployed. One way of ensuring that this does not happen is to design payment schemes that put a premium on placing the most difficult clients.

Governments are also faced with a dilemma as to how assistance programmes should be adapted to operate in the context of unusually high unemployment. For instance, welfare-to-work and similar programmes usually make a number of demands on those seeking help, such as asking them to prove that they are actively looking for a job or progressively reducing benefits the longer a person is out of work. When there are nowhere near enough jobs for the number of applicants, this type of condition may seem pointless and unfair. While some flexibility is required in enforcing these requirements, it is crucial to maintain core job placement services. In fact, employers continue to hire significant numbers of workers, even in a deep recession, and the public employment service should actively assist the unemployed to match up with potential employers.

A "work first" approach is unlikely to be successful for all job losers, because employers can be very selective when many job seekers are competing for a diminished supply of job openings. Other forms of assistance will often be required for less qualified workers. In particular, some shift towards a "train first" approach for more vulnerable workers appears to be required. That is, a more long-term strategy would be adopted for the least employable which aims to improve their skills and chances of finding a job when the economy recovers.

Employment subsidies may also be a useful way to offset the worst impacts of the crisis on employment. These could take several forms. Most straightforwardly, the government can offer subsidies to firms that expand employment, where the subsidy can be limited to hires of disadvantaged workers. Many countries operate such schemes, often targeting them at youth, older workers or the long-term unemployed.

Temporary reductions in employers' social security contributions may be effective in encouraging firms to hire in the short term. One downside is that there would be enormous pressure to apply the reduction to all jobs, not just newly created ones or those at risk. In the longer term, higher taxes may be needed to make up the loss of revenue from reduced charges.

Subsidies for short-time working may prevent job losses and compensate for loss of income. Such schemes can be effective if they are temporary and target firms where demand has fallen temporarily or workers who would have difficulty finding another job. Indeed, a number of European countries, including Germany and the Netherlands, have aggressively expanded short-time work in response to the crisis and this appears to have contributed to keeping the increase in unemployment small relative to how sharply GDP has fallen. While this is encouraging, experience shows that it is essential to wind these programmes down rapidly when the recovery begins, since otherwise they become a brake upon necessary structural change.

All forms of subsidies, and employment subsidies and temporary reductions in social security contributions in particular, risk benefiting individuals who would have been hired anyway, unless the measures are targeted at helping those most in need. For instance, subsidies for all youth would result in employers choosing the most qualified, who would have been hired anyway as soon as job creation resumed, rather than the least skilled who face the risk of drifting into long-term unemployment heightened by the crisis.

Public sector job creation schemes are frequently used to expand employment in recessions. For example, the stimulus packages in a number of countries contain infrastructure and other green growth initiatives that should pay a "double dividend" – lowering unemployment and contributing to the transition towards a low-carbon economy. However, experience shows that it is very difficult for direct job creation schemes to provide a road back to stable employment for disadvantaged workers while also producing socially valuable goods and services.

While the ultimate goal is to reintegrate the unemployed into productive employment, it is also essential to provide adequate income support to job losers in the meantime. The crisis has revealed gaps and shortcomings in unemployment insurance schemes, particularly regarding "non-standard" workers on temporary and short-term contracts. Governments have extended coverage and lengthened the time benefits are paid. Even so, many people are still not covered, and social assistance and income-support schemes require extra funding to help families threatened with poverty.

Governments appear to have learned from past mistakes in treating unemployment. In particular, they have resisted the temptation to encourage early retirement for older job losers and to expand access to long-term sickness or disability schemes for job losers with health problems. These schemes were abject failures in the past, often condemning workers to a life of inactivity whether they wanted it or not, and demographic ageing will make these policies unviable in the long term. The right approach is to make sure that these groups have adequate income support coupled with assistance to become re-employed.

Likewise, it is important to prevent large numbers of young people losing contact with the labour market or being condemned to low-skill, low-wage, dead-end jobs. They should have access to training and other job services even if they don't qualify for unemployment benefits.

Timely, targeted, temporary

Governments moved away from major interventions in, and regulation of, many markets in recent years and have made attempts to promote flexibility in the labour market. That said, the present crisis shows that they have a major role to play when things go wrong. Most OECD countries moved promptly to provide extra resources for labour market programmes early in the downturn, and kept up their efforts as the months passed and the jobs crisis persisted.

However, the pressure to cut large fiscal deficits means governments have to make hard choices on how to allocate scarcer public resources. Given the seriousness of the impacts on the labour market and the associated social and economic risks, a strong case can be made for labour market programmes. But it becomes essential to focus on cost-effective programmes and to target the most disadvantaged groups at risk of losing contact with the labour market.

Special measures to help workers weather a deep recession should be characterised by the "Three T's": timely, targeted and temporary.

Timely: People who have lost their jobs and seen their income suddenly and drastically reduced need help quickly. Income support and services that help in finding a new job need more resources to meet rapidly expanding demand.

Targeted: Resources will be limited, so they have to be used where they can do the most good. This is straightforward for income support, but much more delicate for job services. Policy makers have to decide if it's better to target those who can be found jobs more easily, or disadvantaged workers who need much more training and other kinds of help.

Temporary: Structural labour market reforms contributed to the high levels of employment seen before the crisis. It may be necessary to adapt some practices to cope with recessionary conditions, and the crisis may reveal the need for some permanent changes. Nonetheless, any changes should not stay in place if they hold back employment prospects once the recovery begins.

Find Out More

OECD

On the Internet

For more on employment issues at the OECD, visit *www.oecd.org/employment*.

For OECD statistics, go to *http://stats.OECD.org*.

Publications

OECD Employment Outlook 2010: Moving beyond the Jobs Crisis: The OECD's annual report on employment and labour markets in the OECD area and beyond examines the immediate policy challenges and provides advice for OECD governments. A first chapter sets out the facts and figures related to recent employment developments and sets them in the broader economic context, The *Outlook* analyses three specific policy areas: the jobs impact and policy response in emerging economies; institutional and policy determinants of labour market flows; and the quality of part-time work. The volume closes with a statistical annex which provides the latest available employment data

OECD Insights: International Migration, Keeley, B. (2009): Drawing on the unique expertise of the OECD, this book moves beyond rhetoric to look at the realities of international migration today: Where do migrants come from and where do they go? How do governments manage migration? How well do migrants perform in education and in the workforce? And does migration help – or hinder – developing countries?

International Migration Outlook: SOPEMI 2010: This publication examines the economic crisis and its impact on international migration, describes how flows and migration policy have been recently affected by the crisis, and analyses the forecast medium- and long-term impact. Two special chapters address the determinants of public opinion regarding migration, and the impact of naturalisation on the labour market outcomes of immigrants, exploring how acquisition of citizenship can increase opportunities.

Jobs for Youth: This series includes, for each subject country: an examination of the school-to-work transition process, a survey of the main barriers to employment for young people, an assessment of the adequacy and effectiveness of existing measures to improve the transition from school-to-work, and a set of policy recommendations for further action by the public authorities and social partners.

Also of interest

Tackling the Jobs Crisis, OECD Labour and Employment Ministerial Meeting website *(www.oecd.org/employment/ministerial)*: The OECD Employment and Labour Ministers met in September 2009 to discuss how best labour market and social policies can help workers and low-income households weather the storm of the crisis. Several interesting background reports are available: "Helping youth to get a firm foothold in the labour market", "Maintaining the activation stance during the crisis" and "The Jobs Crisis: What are the implications for employment and social policy?"

5

Pension fund assets dropped by over $5 trillion from $27 trillion during the crisis. The losses to benefits as a consequence will not affect all participants in pension funds equally, with older workers suffering most, while those in defined-benefit plans will probably be better off. Even before the crisis, though, there were calls to reform pensions.

Pensions and
the Crisis

By way of introduction ...

After the Deepwater Horizon oil platform exploded in the Gulf of Mexico with the loss of 11 lives, global attention focused on what would turn out to be the worst environmental disaster in US history. As the weeks went by and attempts to stop the leak failed, the costs of the cleanup plus potential damages began to mount, and markets became increasingly nervous about BP.

The UK media started to highlight another aspect of the story, typified by this headline in the *Daily Express* on 2 June 2010: "BP oil disaster sinks our pensions".

The previous day, the BBC's business editor Robert Peston had explained: "Given that BP is a core holding of most British pension funds, [BP's £40 billion drop in market value] is tens of billions of pounds off the wealth of millions of British people saving for a pension. And with BP dividends representing around 8% of all income going into those pension funds (and a considerably higher proportion of all corporate dividends received by those funds), if BP's oil spill in the Gulf of Mexico causes collateral damage to its dividend-paying capacity, well, many of us will be feeling a bit poorer."

The case illustrates how pension funds are an integral part of the economic life of OECD countries and the people who live in them. Most workers are, or will be, affected by rises or falls in pension values, while with trillions of dollars in assets, their size makes the funds a major influence on world financial markets. They are heavily involved in the real economy too. Pension funds invest across a wide range of businesses as a way to reduce their vulnerability to shocks – including major ones like BP – and assure their long-term profitability.

But they are not all-powerful. The collapse of financial markets that would trigger the Great Recession had immediate effects on pension fund assets, wiping out in a few months the gains built up over years. This prompted concern that people would lose their pension or receive far less than they had expected.

▶ Are these fears justified, and what should be done to prevent a similar situation arising in the future? This chapter looks at the impact of the financial crisis on different groups of workers and pensioners and examines which countries are the worst affected. It also discusses possible government actions to help those already suffering, and to make sure future benefits are protected.

What happened?

Pension funds were worth around $27 trillion in 2007 just before the crisis. Total world GDP at the time was $55 trillion according to the World Bank. Around half the funds' investments were in the property market and corporate bonds and deposits. After rising steadily for the previous five years, stock markets collapsed in 2008, as did property markets, and the value of pension fund assets fell by $3.5 trillion. Not all values suffered. With stock markets panicking and fears that the whole system could implode, dull but dependable government bonds started to look like an attractive proposition. The world government bond index increased by around 7% over 2008.

The overall figure for pension funds' losses hides significant variations from one country and one fund to another, depending on the contents of their portfolios.

Ireland, with a loss of nearly 38%, and Australia, with 27%, showed the worst investment performance in 2008. The United States, which accounts for around a half of all private-pension assets in OECD countries, showed the third largest decline: around 26%. Values fell by more than 20% in another five countries – Belgium, Canada, Hungary, Iceland and Japan.

Losses were only around 10% in Germany, the Slovak Republic, Norway, Spain and Switzerland, and smaller still in the Czech Republic and Mexico. The main reason some funds did better was they invested mainly in bonds, especially government bonds. Equities represented only 6% to 12% in portfolios in the Czech and Slovak Republics, Germany and Mexico, for example. However, it is important to remember that over the long term, equities have delivered larger (though riskier) returns.

Thanks to the rebound in equity prices that started in March 2009, pension funds in some OECD countries completely recovered from their 2008 losses (Austria, Chile, Hungary, Iceland, New Zealand, Norway, and Poland). Pension funds in OECD countries recovered around $1.5 trillion of the $3.5 trillion they lost in 2008. Despite this, total asset values in the OECD area were still 9% below the December 2007 levels on average.

Funding levels for pension funds were still significantly lower at the end of 2009 than two years previously. The gap between assets and liabilities was 26% at the end of 2009, compared with 23% a year earlier, and only 13% in 2007 before the crisis. Decreasing bond yields (which are used to calculate liabilities) in many countries meant that liabilities went up, offsetting the investment recovery.

PENSION FUNDS' REAL INVESTMENT RETURNS, 2008

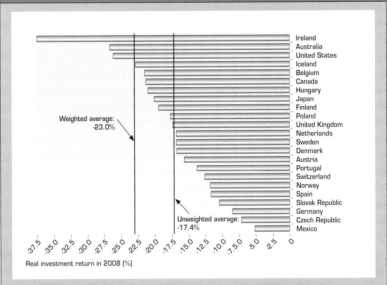

The figure shows investment returns of pension funds in real terms (allowing for inflation) for the 2008 calendar year. Data are presented for 23 OECD countries where private pension funds are large relative to the economy (with assets worth at least 4% of national income at the end of 2007). The weighted average real return – of minus 23% – reflects the importance of the United States in the figures. The unweighted average (including each of the 23 countries equally) was minus 17%.

Source: Pensions at a Glance 2009.

StatLink ᴍᴤ🔗 *http://dx.doi.org/10.1787/888932320637*

Public pension reserve funds in some countries were hit badly by the financial crisis during 2008, but they recovered strongly in 2009, largely making up for the losses. By the end of 2009, the total amount of their assets was equivalent to $4.5 trillion, on average 7.3% higher than at the end of 2008, and 13.9% higher than in December 2007.

The funds that rode out the crisis best were those with conservative investment portfolios.

Who suffered most?

Most pension funds were wealthy enough to survive the crisis and wait for things to improve. However, some people paying into them were hit twice, losing their savings because of the financial crash, then losing their job as the crisis in financial markets started to take its toll on the rest of the economy. This is particularly serious for older workers, who have less time to build up savings again, and have more trouble finding a new job.

Public pension schemes are affected too, and again they could be hit twice. First, because their investments may be worth less. Second, unemployment and lower earnings mean less money is flowing into the system, but unless the rules are changed, it still has to pay out just as much as before.

Even if pension funds are already recovering, for individuals, the effects could be devastating, and permanent. Different countries have different setups, but figures for US 401(k) plans discussed in the next section (named after a clause in the tax code) show broad characteristics found elsewhere.

As mentioned above, age is the first factor in determining the impact of the crisis, and type of pension plan the second.

Particularly hard for older workers

Older workers face the worst impacts. The balances in private pension accounts of younger workers are generally small and financial losses in absolute terms are therefore also small compared with other age groups. For 25-34 year-olds with at least five years in the plan, additional contributions made in 2008 outweighed investment losses, with balances increasing by nearly 5%.

For people near to retirement however, investment losses in private pension funds, public pension reserves and other savings may not be recouped. Even postponing their retirement may allow them to offset only part of their loss. Declines in account balances in private pensions in the US were largest for the 45-54 year-old age group, ranging from a loss of around 18% for people with short tenures to 25% for longer periods of coverage.

The degree to which the crisis affects current pensioners depends on the composition of their old-age income. The purchasing power of public pensions is usually protected by automatic indexation arrangements. But in a number of countries, the crisis will have an impact on the level of public pensions as a result of automatic adjustment mechanisms which could result in lower benefits. (We'll discuss this below.) Private pension benefits are also generally protected, as occupational pension plans and annuity providers hold assets to back these benefits. The burden of rectifying shortfalls falls on others, such as employers, financial-service companies, government-backed guarantee programmes and plan contributors.

But any voluntary retirement savings or housing assets that pensioners were hoping to draw on during their retirement are, of course, hit by the crisis. For some pensioners, losses in these assets are substantial and interest rates are at historic lows, which may mean much lower living standards in old age.

Type of plan

Apart from public and private schemes, pension plans are split between two other broad categories: *defined-contribution* and *defined-benefit*.

In defined-contribution plans, each person saves for retirement in an individual account and the value of pension benefits is determined by investment performance. Riskier investments may pay out more when the stock market is booming, but in a financial crisis, they can lose value quickly, leaving people who depended on them poorer than they expected. Again, this doesn't matter so much to younger workers who do not need the income immediately, and who, moreover, may actually benefit by being able to buy assets cheaply and enjoy good returns in the future.

For retirees with defined-contribution plans, the effect of the crisis depends on what they did with the funds in their account at the time of retirement. Many are protected because they purchased an annuity before the crisis, thereby benefiting from a life-long pension payment. The downside, at the time, may have been that they missed out on the high returns when the markets were buoyant. The opposite is the case for those who decided they could live off their dividends, or chose to wait and profit from the high returns for a bit longer.

In defined-benefit plans, pensions should be paid whatever the fund's performance. However, the stock market crash means that the assets that fund the payouts are worth less, and many plans are now in deficit. The UK's biggest defined-benefit plan, that of British Telecom, had a deficit of £9 billion at the end of 2008 (roughly the same as the actual market value of the company), and some estimates say it could be as high as £11 billion. Plans such as this could try to make up the shortfall by increasing contributions or cutting benefits. The BT fund trustees say the deficit should be tackled through annual top-up payments of at least £500 million for 17 years. If the plan is run by a private company and that company goes bankrupt, beneficiaries could end up with nothing, or at best a much smaller sum paid out by government guarantee schemes.

Not only private plans are concerned. A number of studies warn about the situation of public employees' pensions too. A report by US National Public Radio in March 2010 looked at various estimates of the liabilities and assets of state pension funds and calculated how long it would take each state to make good on its pension promises if it spent all its tax revenue on pensions and nothing else. Vermont is best off, but would still take 1.7 years. At the other end of the scale, Ohio and Colorado would have to spend all their revenue on pensions for over eight years to balance the books.

National-level public pension plans are not in such a perilous state. For a start, only eight OECD countries have public pension reserves that were worth more than 5% of national income in 2007, and many countries invest massively in government bonds. These don't pay as much as other investments, but they are a lot safer. The fund in the United States is invested entirely in government bonds, for example, and 80% of the portfolio of Korea's reserve is in bonds. That said, some countries are more exposed to financial market risk. For instance, the government bond share is less than 20% in New Zealand and Ireland.

The crisis will still affect even national funds with risk-averse portfolios though. Unemployment and slower growth reduce the tax and contribution revenues of public pension systems. Demand for payouts could also increase if more workers opt for early retirement to avoid unemployment. Also, the need to finance bailouts and stimulus packages will put public finances under pressure for years to come. Governments have had to borrow to finance stimulus packages and compensate for lost revenue and budget deficits. In 2010, OECD governments are expected to borrow $16 trillion. This will increase pressure to cut pension spending, along with other public programmes.

Automatic stabilisers and destabilisers

Governments influence pension plans in a number of ways through regulation of financial markets and of the funds themselves, as well as through various statutory requirements such as legal retirement age.

The state also intervenes through what are known as "automatic stabilisers".

The overall impact of the crisis on retirement income depends on these stabilisers and anti-poverty safety nets built into countries' pension systems. Most countries have provisions that help prevent retirees from falling into poverty in their old age, which may buffer the impact of investment losses on retirement income for some people. Public retirement-income programmes – basic pensions and earnings-related schemes – will pay the same benefit regardless of the outcome for private pensions.

However, many countries have a set-up in which the amount paid out by the public scheme depends on the resources of the beneficiary and the value of private pensions. The payout is adjusted in line with rises and falls of the private pension. In Australia and Denmark, for example, most current retirees receive resource-tested benefits (more than 75% of older people in Australia and around 65% in Denmark). The value of these entitlements increases as private pensions deliver lower returns, protecting much of the incomes of low- and middle-earners. In Australia, each extra dollar of private pensions results in a 40 cent reduction in public pensions. Conversely, a dollar less in private pensions results in 60 cents more from the public pension.

In these cases, the public retirement-income programmes act as automatic stabilisers, meaning that some or most retirees are shielded from the full impact of the financial crisis on their income in old age. Canada, Germany and Sweden on the other hand have mechanisms in place that automatically adjust benefits to ensure the solvency of the public pension scheme. These could be termed "automatic destabilisers" as they have the reverse effect of the automatic stabilisers described above.

Although they protect the finances of the pension scheme, they do so by varying individual retirement incomes and current workers' accrued benefits. These automatic adjustments – if they are not overridden – might result in reductions in real benefits for current pensioners due to a mix of the effect of the financial crisis on investment and the impact of the economic crisis on earnings and employment.

Two-way influences

So far, we've discussed the immediate interactions between pensions and the crisis, but pension funds, by their very nature, have to work with a long time horizon and their performance should also be evaluated on this basis. Focusing on a single year, good or bad, can be misleading.

The decline in equity returns over 2000-02 was just as serious as in 2008, though the latter has been much faster. Despite the severity and proximity of these two downturns, pension fund performance has been positive over the last ten years and healthy over the last fifteen years.

Most pension funds also have very small liquidity needs (need for "ready cash") in relation to their total assets under management. This means that they do not have to sell assets at current low prices to meet benefit payments and other expenditures, as they can rely on the regular flow of contributions and investment income, even if the latter is reduced. The main exception is plans that rely on running down their assets to meet benefit payouts, so when asset values decline sharply, they cannot wait until the market recovers to sell.

The longer-term outlook depends of course on what happens in the markets. Optimists could argue that the much faster drop in values compared to 2000-02 is a result of closer links in the financial system and that recovery could be just as rapid. Pessimists could point out that unlike today, the previous crash was not followed by a major credit crunch and a deep recession across the developed economies.

Financial markets are a major influence on pensions of course, but with assets worth half world GDP, pension funds have a massive influence on markets too. The funds can be "market stabilisers", smoothing out fluctuations in prices by selling when markets are high and buying when they are low. However, in the latest crisis, certain funds sold part of their equity portfolios ("flight from equities"). In some countries, pension funds have reacted by allocating new pension contributions to bank deposits and other financial products with government guarantees until the situation in capital markets stabilises.

A flight from equities affects defined-contribution plans in countries where participants can choose portfolios. In countries with mandatory systems, investment returns are reported monthly or quarterly, leading many participants to switch to lower-risk portfolios. Such behaviour, while rational from a short-term perspective, ultimately leads to lower pensions than if participants had stuck to their previous asset allocation into the long term. Participants risk missing out on the equity recovery, and if they do decide to get back into equities, face paying much more for shares than previously. That said, it's hard to convince ordinary people that the best strategy is to hold on to their shares and wait for the storm to blow over when they see traders and other professionals selling as quickly as they can.

In defined-benefit plans, a shift in investments away from equities is also likely, though perhaps less pronounced than in defined-contribution plans. One important deciding factor is the implementation of standards and rules governing how funds value assets and liabilities. Governments and trustees insist on an obligatory ratio of reserves to payouts, and define what the fund has to do if reserves fall too low to meet legal requirements. This can mean that the funds have to sell part of their equity holdings, even at a loss, during a downturn.

Funds could react by looking for alternative investments with better returns (for example, hedge funds or speculating on future commodity prices). Many pension funds have been embracing alternative investments in a herd-like way, seeking the higher returns promised by these assets without fully understanding the underlying risks involved.

Some pension funds are also starting to move into the market for loans that fund indebted companies and buy-outs. This market is a potential boost to the lending system dominated by banks and a few investment funds. Certain pension funds have been pursuing a strategy to diversify into credit for a number of years and consider the turmoil as a good buying opportunity. Sometimes, however, the bets have not paid off. For example, ABP, the large Dutch pension fund, may have suffered major losses from an investment in Lehman Brothers made just before its insolvency.

Changes in risk

The way funds try to protect themselves from risk has been complicated by the crisis, and some of the strategies are risky, including derivatives (the reason they pay more than other investments is that the risk is greater). The types of derivatives most used by pension funds are financial instruments that derive their value from interest rates and are traded directly between two parties. This so-called "over the counter" trade does not pass through a regulated exchange and is not monitored or supervised by public authorities. In fact nobody really knows what is happening beyond their own immediate business, and when something goes wrong, as in the case of Lehman, markets panic because of all the uncertainty surrounding who could go under.

One immediate consequence of the market meltdown is a move against short-selling. Short-selling is the practice whereby sellers sell a security they don't actually own yet, in the hope that they can buy it later at a lower price before having to deliver it. Hedge funds, for example, often borrow stocks to implement popular strategies based on expected price differences of the stocks. Financial market regulators have restricted short-selling of stocks. Many pension funds have now stopped their stock lending practices since the fees they charged speculators did not justify the risk that they would not recover the value of the stock loaned. The funds also fear that they may have contributed to the financial crisis through these lending practices.

An extremely complicated situation has been made even worse by developments in bond markets. Government bonds don't pay much compared with other investments, and they tie up funds for anything up to 40 years, but they are seen as a safe bet. Or rather they were. Worries about sovereign debt, plus the sheer amount of bonds governments issued in the wake of the crisis, have made them a much less attractive long-term option for investors, including pension funds.

Apart from investment risk, pension funds, especially defined-benefit ones, have to deal with another, longer-term "risk": longevity. People are living longer and thus receiving payouts for a longer time. Nobody really knows how longevity will evolve in the future. On the one hand, actuaries have tended to underestimate future gains, while on the other, some demographers claim that the obesity epidemic could actually halt or even reverse the increases among some groups of the population. Historical evidence suggests that a continuing increase seems the most likely path, with direct consequences for the pensions industry. An article in *The Economist* in February 2010 reported that every additional year of life expectancy at age 65 increases the present value of pension liabilities in British defined-benefit schemes by 3%, or £30 billion ($48 billion). Total exposure to longevity risk in the UK is estimated at over £2 trillion by the Life and Longevity Markets Association (LLMA).

The traditional way of dealing with this was to sell the liabilities to a firm that agreed to run the pension scheme for a premium, but the expanding deficits in funds caused by the crisis have made this solution less attractive to buyers, and too expensive in many cases. One way of dealing with this risk may be "longevity swaps": the pension fund pays another party an agreed revenue stream (so much per year or month) and receives an income that rises if longevity is higher than expected.

However, this idea is not likely to prove very attractive in situations of great uncertainty and concerns over risk. The LLMA, launched in London in February 2010 by a group of banks and insurers, hopes to tackle the issue by creating a separate market for this risk.

Policy responses

Work longer?

In past recessions, governments have used early retirement or entitlement to disability benefits first to protect the incomes of older workers who lose their jobs and are unable to find another, and second to keep unemployment figures down. This approach has short-term advantages (not least for the workers in question) but the long-term impact on labour markets is negative because it is difficult to undo the impacts of these policies even when the initial justification no longer exists.

In countries with large and relatively mature defined-contribution pension systems people may wish to work longer to repair their retirement savings. In theory, this would add extra contributions; reduce the number of years of retirement the pension finances; and allow time for asset values to recover. In practice, older workers may find it hard to get a job and the recovery in asset prices might be too far off to make a difference, so a social safety-net may be their only source of extra income.

More choice?

Individuals can choose their investment portfolio in most defined-contribution pension plans, and their choices have important implications for the effect of the crisis on their pensions. Data for the United States show that people tend to shift away from equities towards less risky investments as they approach retirement. For example, around 55% of 36-45 year-olds hold more than 70% of their portfolios in equities, falling to 43% of people age 56 to 65. Yet despite the tendency to go for less risky investments, the portfolio share of equities of workers close to retirement seems very high: more than one in five hold more than 90% of their 401(k)s in equities. Of course they may hold lower-risk deposits and bonds outside of their 401(k)s, but these workers will have seen their pension savings significantly eroded relative to the minority who held most of their portfolios in lower-risk assets.

What are the implications of this type of investment behaviour for policy? Should people be restricted in their choices to prevent them from having their old-age savings wiped out? Or should this be an individual decision and a risk to take at people's own discretion?

At the least, government should encourage individuals to adopt a strategy towards less risk as they approach retirement. Often called life-cycle investing, this strategy can reduce investment risk over a person's career without sacrificing the benefits from a broader portfolio at younger ages. There is a case for making this shift automatic, and making it the default option. Using a life-cycle approach as a default puts investments on "automatic pilot" and is especially useful for individuals who do not want to manage their portfolio actively. This is probably the majority of people in most countries. In fact, a survey by the Royal Bank of Canada found that respondents consider choosing the right investments for a retirement savings plan to be more stressful than going to the dentist.

An automatic pilot policy can be adopted while preserving individual choice between portfolios with different risk-return characteristics (for the minority who do want to take their own investment decisions).

Allowing people who opted for private plans back into public ones is another possibility. This is tempting for governments to help tackle deficits in public pension systems, and for workers afraid of substantial losses from private plans. However, the gains are likely to be only short term, and there would be calls to switch back again when the economy picks up.

Should governments bail out private pensions?

Should governments bail out individuals' pension accounts as they did for the banks? Governments already stand behind many countries' occupational, defined-benefit schemes. Governments may have a moral, if not a statutory, duty to help where defined-contribution pensions are mandatory rather than voluntary and annuitisation at retirement is obligatory. A direct bailout, paying money into people's pension accounts, could prove to be very expensive, and possibly not feasible anyway when the public finances are being squeezed by recession and economic-stimulus packages.

Providing support to the retirement savings of those most affected by the crisis through the public pension system would have the advantage of spreading the cost over time. The payments would be made over the period of an individual's retirement rather than in one go either now or at the time of retirement. This would also allow for greater efficiency and flexibility: support could be targeted towards low-income retirees, for example.

A bailout would make most sense for people who are close to pension age. However, this poses political difficulties. If it were restricted to people within a few years of normal pension age, then workers slightly younger than the cut-off age would feel cheated. Similarly, retirees who annuitised their pension only recently, locking in financial market losses, would complain if contemporaries who kept their money in financial markets were to be compensated.

There is also a risk of "moral hazard" resulting from a direct bailout of pension funds: the expectation of a bailout next time something goes wrong will encourage people to behave more riskily once the current crisis is over.

What should be done?

Even before the 2008 crisis, there had been warnings about the need to reform private pensions. The OECD has been calling for stronger pension fund governance since the publication of a set of guidelines in 2001, which are currently being revised. The guidelines stress the need for effective monitoring of investment risks and performance and of the relationship between pension funds' assets and liabilities. Greater expertise and knowledge are required on pension fund boards, including the appointment of independent experts.

The OECD has highlighted the interplay between scale and governance. Small pension funds are more prone to weak governance (and they are much more expensive to manage and supervise), so there is a strong case to consolidate the pension fund sector through mergers in some countries.

Regulatory reform of both defined-benefit and defined-contribution systems should also be on the policy agenda. Some regulations intended to protect participants of defined-benefit plans may actually make things worse by reinforcing the downward spiral in asset values. Even in a severe crisis, investors do not lose anything on an investment until they sell it at less than they paid for it originally (or the company goes out of business). Yet in some countries, the rules do not allow funds to sit out a crisis and wait for values to rise again. They have to sell to maintain asset to liability ratios, and given the major role pension funds play in some markets, this drives prices down even further.

The crisis will lead to further closures of defined-benefit plans as funding gaps widen and contribution requirements increase. Insolvency guarantee funds will also be active over the next couple of years bailing out the pension funds sponsored by bankrupt companies. As the defined-benefit pension sector shrinks further, the possible role of regulations in reinforcing this trend should be examined.

For defined-contribution plans, responses could include appropriate default mechanisms and the design of "autopilot" funds that shift towards lower risk investments as retirement date approaches without the beneficiary having to intervene. A key goal of this regulation is to reduce the "timing risk" of transforming an accumulated balance into a regular benefit stream (an annuity).

Governments should also consider the suitability of different investment strategies as default options, taking into account the extent of choice in the payout stage, the generosity of the public pension system and the level of contributions, among other factors. Default investment strategies should be evaluated as to how adequate and predictable retirement income is.

Better policy design is also needed for the pension pay-out phase of defined-contribution systems. Some of the mandatory and default arrangements in place are far from safe and fail to integrate the accumulation and retirement stage in a coherent manner. In particular, making the purchase of annuities mandatory makes most sense in countries where public pension benefits are low. However, forcing individuals to purchase annuities goes against principles of free choice and may impose heavy costs on individuals when annuity rates are low or account balances have dropped as a result of bad market conditions.

A more flexible approach that could be introduced as a default option for the pension pay-out phase is to combine "phased withdrawals", where a defined part of the fund balance can be withdrawn each year, with deferred annuities that start paying benefits after a certain age, such as 85. Such deferred annuities could be bought at the time of retirement with a small part of the accumulated balance.

In the context of the financial crisis and the rapid growth of defined-contribution plans in many countries, effective financial education programmes and information disclosure are very important to the functioning of the private pension system. Policy initiatives in this area should complement the regulations on investment choice and default options that already exist in some countries. As workers take more responsibility for saving for their own retirement, the role of governments changes, but it remains of paramount importance to promote the adequacy and security of old-age income.

The crisis hasn't reduced the importance of private pensions in a well-balanced system. Private pensions are necessary to diversify the sources of income at retirement and, as such, they complement public pensions. Moreover, the sustainability problems facing public pensions in some countries remain challenging, and could get worse as the workforce ages. As a result of the large projected increases in public pension expenditures in the near future, retirement income from public sources is expected to continue to decline, and therefore private pensions need to be expanded further to bolster income in retirement.

A long-term issue	

A simulation using 25 years of data on investment returns for the G7 economies and Sweden shows a real annual return of 5.5% for bonds and 9.0% for equities over the 45-year horizon of a full career's pension savings. For a "balanced" portfolio – half in equities and half in bonds – the average (median) return is 5.0%.

The analysis also investigates the scale of risk and uncertainty over investment returns. In the worst 10% of cases, for example, returns are expected to be just 3.2% a year or less. In the best 10% of cases, annual returns are 6.7% or more.

However, the simulations are based on around 25 years of data, ending in 2006. The period since then includes both substantially negative returns on equities and much greater volatility. The equity market crash of 1987, included in the data, saw prices fall as much as in 2008. Also, the end of the technology-stock bubble, which led to substantial stock-market falls in 2000-02, is in the time period covered.

The outlook

Poverty rates of older people have fallen over the past three decades and children and young adults (people age 25 or under) have replaced older people as a group with a relatively high risk of poverty. The major social and economic change that will affect future incomes of older people is the changing role of women: greater labour-market participation, a narrowing gender pay gap and better protection for periods of childcare leave.

Pension reforms will also have a substantial impact on the evolution of old-age incomes and poverty. Countries that have cut benefits across the board are likely to see lower pensioner incomes and greater poverty in the future, unless individuals make up for these cuts by working longer or with voluntary retirement savings.

Average old-age incomes may well fall in countries that protected low earners from cuts, but this policy means that pensioner poverty will not be affected by reform.

In the countries that moved to a stronger pension-earnings link, average incomes of the old may increase, but overall pensioner poverty may be higher due to the lack of redistribution in the new pension systems.

Finally, the group that increased mandatory retirement provision should naturally see higher incomes in old age. In all of these cases, the changes will help low earners more, and so there should be a larger effect on pensioner poverty.

Quantitative easing

The economic crisis has seen some obscure financial jargon pass into everyday language, subprime being the most infamous example. Quantitative easing is unlikely to gain similar notoriety, but as a measure that could have major implications for pensions, it is worth examining.

In April 2009, the average interest rate set by the central banks of the G7 nations fell to 0.5%. What happens when money is so cheap it can't get any cheaper? In other words, what can you do when interest rates can no longer be cut because they are so low already?

Quantitative easing is one possibility. The central bank injects money into the economy by buying certain financial products, notably government bonds (also known as gilts). The sellers are expected to use the money to lend to businesses and households or to invest (although they may just leave it in bank deposits or send it offshore). The US Federal Reserve applied quantitative easing during the banking crisis that followed the 1929 Wall Street Crash, and the Bank of Japan adopted a similar approach to dealing with the crisis in the 1990s following the crash of the property market.

The media often present this as "the government printing money". The reason is that, instead of borrowing money in the usual way by issuing new bonds, the government, through the central bank, simply creates the money and uses it to pay the banks and other financial institutions it intends to help.

.../...

Quantitative easing (continued)

What does this mean for pensions? As such, it is bad news. If quantitative easing succeeds in making government bonds more attractive, the interest paid on these bonds does not have to be as high as it was previously. Pension funds are massive holders of government bonds, so a drop in the interest paid on them (the yield) translates directly into a loss of income to the funds. And since the pensions industry uses bond yields to calculate pension payments such as annuity income, pensioners will be affected.

Company pension schemes could be affected too. The yield on government bonds is an important element in calculating the future liability of pension funds, and when yields fall, liability increases. Moreover, pension scheme trustees generally estimate pension liabilities in terms of the price of gilts, so at the same time as yields are falling, liabilities are increasing.

Some industry analysts are afraid that the life insurance and pensions industry could become the victim of a fall in the yield from government bonds, combined with a significant increase in the number of companies defaulting on the debt that many pension funds bought, as well as a drop in the value of the stocks pension funds invested in.

The immediate outlook for pension funds is gloomy, and deflation could make it even worse. Deflation could, however, be good news for some pensioners. The reason is that in many schemes, the fund has to increase payments to offset inflation (at least partly), but few, if any, have a mechanism to reduce payments when there is deflation.

Sources: Bank of England, *Provisional estimates of narrow money (notes & coin) and reserve balances;* Deloitte LLP (2009), *Quantitative easing contributes to FTSE 100 pension scheme deficits increasing to £180bn.*

Find Out More

OECD

On the Internet

For an introduction to OECD work on pensions, see *www.oecd.org/pensions.*

Publications

Pensions at a Glance 2009: Retirement-Income Systems in OECD Countries (2009): This report provides information on key features of pension provision in OECD countries and projections of retirement income for today's workers. It offers an extensive range of indicators, including measures of assets, investment performance, coverage of private pensions, public pension spending, and the demographic context and outlook.

The Political Economy of Reform: Lessons from Pensions, Product Markets and Labour Markets in Ten OECD Countries (2009): By examining 20 structural reform efforts in 10 OECD countries over the past two decades, this report examines why some policy reforms get implemented and others languish. The case studies cover a wide variety of reform attempts including pensions. The report's two-pronged analytical approach – quantitative and qualitative – results in unique insights for policy makers designing, adopting and implementing policy reforms.

OECD Private Pensions Outlook 2008: This book guides readers through the changing landscape of retirement income provision. This edition presents a special feature on the implications of the financial crisis for private pensions, as well as in-depth, international analyses of private pension arrangements across OECD and selected non-OECD countries. The publication focuses on the role of pension funds, and also provides evidence on public pension reserve funds which complement the financing of social security systems.

Improving Financial Education and Awareness on Insurance and Private Pensions (2008): With public pensions under pressure and private pensions exposed to risk, individuals face an increasing variety of financial risks, particularly those linked to their retirement. This book analyzes the level of risk awareness of consumers and highlights good practices governments might initiate to enhance consumers' awareness and education on insurance and private pensions issues.

Also of interest

Private Pensions and Policy Responses to the Financial and Economic Crisis by Antolin, P. and F. Stewart (2009), OECD Working Papers on Insurance and Private Pensions, No. 36, OECD Publishing.

6

In the eyes of many, the crisis and recession revealed gaping holes in the rules of the global economy. Financial markets are the most obvious target for new regulations, but other areas, too, have come under increasing attention, including tax and even the basic values of capitalism.

New World,
New Rules?

By way of introduction...

Is there – to misquote William Shakespeare – something rotten with the state of capitalism? In the wake of the financial crisis, many people seemed to think there was. According to a poll of people in 27 countries commissioned by the BBC World Service, only around one in ten believed capitalism worked well. In just two of the surveyed countries did that number rise above one in five – 25% in the United States and 21% in Pakistan.

Unhappy as people were, the poll showed little appetite for throwing out capitalism altogether – fewer than one in four supported that notion. But people want change – reform and regulation that will check capitalism's worst excesses.

That view is shared by many political leaders. In 2009, Germany's Chancellor Angela Merkel and the Netherlands' then-Prime Minister Jan Peter Balkenende argued that "it is clear that over the past few decades, as the financial system has globalised at unprecedented speed, the various systems of rules and supervision have not kept pace". In the United States, President Barack Obama declared that "we need strong rules of the road to guard against the kind of systemic risks that we've seen". In the United Kingdom, former Prime Minister Gordon Brown said that "instead of a globalisation that threatens to become values-free and rules-free, we need a world of shared global rules founded on shared global values".

▶ What form should those rules and values take? How can we best harness capitalism's power to deliver innovation and satisfy our material needs while minimising its tendency to go off the rails from time to time. This chapter looks at some of the themes that have emerged in reform and regulation since the crisis began, focusing on three main areas:

➤ regulating financial markets;

➤ tackling tax evasion;

➤ creating a "global standard" for ethical behaviour.

Why do we need to regulate financial markets?

In ancient Rome, the judge Lucius Cassius was called on to deal with some complex cases. To get to the bottom of an investigation, he was known for asking a simple, single question: *Cui bono?* Who benefits? Two millennia on, and in a different context, that's a question that's being asked of the global financial system.

At one level we all benefit from the financial system. Without institutions like banks, our complex modern economies couldn't exist: they are at the heart of the payments system, they are safe places to store money, and they bridge the gap between those with money to lend and those needing a loan. Similarly, without share markets, companies would struggle to raise funds; without commodities markets, buyers would lack certainty on future prices of essential goods; without foreign exchange systems, international trade would grind to a halt.

But that's not to say we all benefit from everything financial markets do. For instance, financial markets facilitate speculation – in other words, the buying and selling of assets with the aim of turning a quick profit, rather than holding on to them as a long-term investment. In itself, that's not necessarily bad: speculation means there's almost always someone willing to buy or sell in a market, ensuring much-needed liquidity. But it can have serious downsides if it artificially inflates asset prices. Once formed, such bubbles have a tendency to pop.

In recent decades, speculation has grown hugely on the back of "financial innovations", such as the collateralised debt obligations (CDOs) and credit-default swaps (CDSs) we encountered in Chapter 2. Proponents argue that these allow risk to be greatly diversified – in other words, investors don't need to keep all their risks in one basket. However, Paul Volcker, former chairman of the Federal Reserve, the United States' central bank, has said he can think of only one financial innovation in recent decades that has benefited society – the ATM.

Advances in technology used by financial markets have also come under scrutiny. For example, computer trading allows shares and financial derivatives to be bought and sold in just 300 microseconds – faster than the blink of an eye. Traders use such systems to take advantage of minuscule shifts in prices on markets. On a single bond or share, for instance, this might be nothing more than a decimal point followed by a string of zeroes and a one. But when it's combined across an order worth a million or a hundred million dollars it adds up. *Cui bono?* Proponents say, again, that such approaches increase liquidity in markets. Others are not so sure: "It remains hard to believe that it all adds anything much to the efficiency with which the real economy generates and improves our standard of living," the Nobel laureate Robert Solow has commented.

Some observers have spoken of a division in the financial system: on the one hand are activities that are necessary and that bring wider economic benefits; on the other is something that some critics say resembles a casino. (Although to be fair to casinos, at least risks there are evenly distributed and can be accurately calculated; that's not true of financial markets.) Whether or not that metaphor is fair, there does appear to be little doubt that the financial system in its current form is contributing to financial insecurity: just think of the financial meltdown and a raft of previous incidents, such as the 1997 Asian crisis and the dotcom bubble of the late 1990s. Weakened economies can't afford another meltdown: new rules are needed.

What regulation should aim to achieve

How would a reregulated financial system look? The Financial Stability Board, an international forum for national financial authorities that was created out of a smaller grouping (the Financial Stability Forum) in the wake of the crisis, has set down what it sees as three key objectives:

Objective 1 – Make financial systems less pro-cyclical: As Chapter 3 explained, economies usually move in cycles – some growth followed by a slowdown and then some more growth. One way to think of these ups and downs is in terms of a child sitting quietly on a swing, swinging to and fro. But what happens if she's the adventurous type? Chances are she'll lean forward as the swing goes up and back as it heads down. She may not know the term, but the child is behaving "pro-cyclically" – she's amplifying the swing's oscillation. It's all good fun – until she falls off.

Something similar has happened in the relationship between financial systems and the real economy. During the good times, banks became ever more willing to lend, often to people who once wouldn't have had a chance of getting a loan. That helped fuel a bubble in property prices. But when the good times ended, the lending stopped. (As the poet Robert Frost said, "A bank is a place where they lend you an umbrella in fair weather and ask for it back when it begins to rain.") Businesses that were beginning to struggle during the slowdown suddenly faced an extra problem: they couldn't borrow money. That only increased the risk of failure, adding to the general economic malaise. Just like the little girl pushing the swing forwards and backwards, the financial system can deepen the natural ups and downs of the economy. As a result, the falls are harder than they might otherwise be.

Revised regulations will aim to dampen this effect. For example, they could work to make it harder for banks to lend in the good times but easier in the tough times. This could be done by changing banks' capital requirements. As Chapter 2 explained, in simple terms the amount a bank can lend is restricted by how much capital it has – a bank with a bigger capital buffer can lend more, one with a smaller buffer can lend less. New rules might require banks to build up buffers during an economic upturn, but allow them to fall back to a minimum level when the economy cools.

Objective 2 – Restrict leverage: Leverage, which essentially means borrowing to invest, derives its name from one of the great human discoveries – the lever. To understand how it works, we need to go back to the playground. After the little girl has finished swinging, she runs over to a seesaw (a lever) and sits on one end. Her dad goes to the other end. With just a light push on his end of the seesaw, his little girl at the other end rises effortlessly. That's the power of leverage – a small effort can give a big result. The idea is the same in economics – you borrow a little money (or a lot) and invest it so smartly that the return easily covers the cost of the original loan and provides you with a handsome bonus.

In good times, leverage can be a powerful way to build wealth. But when the economy turns, it can wipe out capital and create huge debts. And that's what happened to the banks during the financial crisis. For years, they found ways to increase their leverage and invested in complex instruments like mortgage-backed securities. The use of offshore subsidiaries and complex transactions meant this build-up of leverage was often not clear on banks' balance sheets. That meant the scale of banks' risk-taking wasn't understood by regulators and investors – and, sometimes, even by bank directors. As mortgage foreclosures spread in the United States and elsewhere, banks' investments became increasingly questionable. That was bad, but the situation was exacerbated by the scale of their leverage.

How does leverage work?

In financial markets, the term "leverage" is used in a couple of different ways. Still, in basic terms leverage always exposes investors to greater risk. "If the bet goes right, the returns are huge; if it goes wrong, the losses are big too," as the journalist Gillian Tett has written.

Leverage doesn't operate only in the rarefied world of high finance. Ordinary people use it, too. Imagine two friends, cautious Claire and leveraged Leo. Claire has just inherited $100 000 in her granny's will, and decides to buy a house for just that amount (as she's borrowing nothing, her leverage ratio is 0). Leo, not wanting to be left behind, decides he'll buy the neighbouring house, but he has savings – or capital – of just $10 000. He goes to his bank, explains the situation, and is delighted when they offer him a $90 000 mortgage at an annual interest rate of 5% (giving him a leverage ratio of around 9 to 1).

A year goes by, the property market has boomed, and the two friends decide to cash in on their houses, each now selling for $130 000. On her initial investment of $100 000, Claire has earned an extra $30 000 – a nice bonus of 30%. What about Leo? Out of his $130 000, he has to pay back his $90 000 loan to his bank plus $4 500 to cover a year's interest payments. Once that's done, he's left with $25 500 (plus the $10 000 he started with) – a whopping bonus of 255%.

But what happens if prices fall? Imagine after a year that the houses are selling for only $70 000. The two friends decide to get out of the market as quickly as possible rather than risking further losses. Against her initial investment of $100 000, cautious Claire now has $70 000; in other words, 70% of her capital remains intact. For leveraged Leo, things are much, much worse. At the end of the year, he owes his bank $94 500 for its loan and the interest on it. Selling the house for only $70 000 means he's still $24 500 short of what he needs, plus he's wiped out his initial capital. In effect, he's bankrupt.

Managing risk

That's why banks' leverage ratios need to be targeted in new financial regulation. But there also needs to be an intense focus on why banks allowed themselves to build up such huge risks in the first place and, more generally, how they manage risk. In theory, banks had all the tools – such as highly complex mathematical models – they needed to do this. In practice, risk management failed. To some extent this was a technical issue – those computer models may have been complex but they weren't always right. But it was also a human issue. Examples of this are myriad. In many banks, risk managers didn't – and still don't – enjoy nearly the same status as high-flying traders, so they were easily overshadowed, ignored and sometimes co-opted by better-paid trading teams keen on pushing the risk envelope. Executive pay was also a factor *(see box)*.

> "Testimony by the ex-head of risk at the British bank **HBOS** … gives a picture of a bank management with little regard or care for risk management as it pursued its headlong rush into expanding its mortgage business."
>
> Grant Kirkpatrick, *OECD Journal: Financial Market Trends*

There were also very serious failures of corporate governance. Directors did not always receive realistic risk assessments, or were not informed of strategic decisions taken by managers regarding risk exposure. Even when they did receive the relevant information, they didn't always understand it. That's worrying, but it's also not surprising: modern financial markets are hugely complex, and there's a real shortage of people who can fully get to grips with them, not just at the board level but also at the management level. There were also failures to heed warnings. For instance, directors of the failed Northern Rock bank in the United Kingdom admitted reading official reports in early 2007 warning of liquidity risks (in simple terms, this is where a bank doesn't have the funds to meet immediate demands), but did nothing about them.

Revised regulation will need to impose stricter standards of corporate governance, but that can go only so far. There will also need to be a real sea change in attitudes and an acceptance by directors both of the seriousness of their task and of their responsibility to shareholders, creditors and wider society. The former CEO of Unilever, Niall Fitzgerald, who has also served as a bank director, sees the challenge facing directors before the crisis – as well as today – in this way: "The question you have to ask yourselves is: did you know what the institution was doing and the full consequences of what it was doing? Because, if you did, you were complicit with the recklessness. Or if the answer is you didn't know, then you cannot have been discharging your responsibility as a director of the company properly."

Objective 3 – Penalise mistakes: It's one of the ironies of the financial crisis that an era in which banks and financial institutions enjoyed ever greater freedom to regulate themselves ended in massive state intervention. To outsiders looking in, it can seem that financial institutions were happy to push the state away as long as they were making money, but once things turned sour they came running for help. That hasn't come cheap for taxpayers: according to OECD estimates, governments have made commitments of over $11 trillion to support troubled banks and financial institutions (note, this represents commitments to cover worst-case scenarios, not actual spending).

Many observers believe this rescue is not a one-off result of the recent financial crisis, but rather part of a long-term trend. After centuries in which the banks came to the aid of the state, "for the past two centuries, the tables have progressively turned. The state has instead become the last-resort financier of the banks," according to a paper co-authored by the Bank of England's Andrew Haldane. Even though states have repeatedly said "never again", his paper says that risks from allowing widespread bank defaults are so great that "such a statement lacks credibility. Knowing this, the rational response by market participants is to double their bets. This adds to the cost of future crises. And the larger these costs, the lower the credibility of 'never again' announcements. This is a doom loop."

Nouriel Roubini, a high-profile economics professor and consultant, and others have described this as "a system where profits are privatized and ... losses socialized" – in other words, in the good times bankers get to keep their winnings, in the bad times taxpayers pick up the tab. Clearly, such a situation raises serious questions of social equity and justice. But even aside from these, the crisis has underlined the role of what's called "moral hazard" – in other words, unless people pay the price of their mistakes there's no incentive for them not to go on making those mistakes.

One problem for governments is that banks have become increasingly vulnerable to failure, but allowing them to collapse has become increasingly dangerous. As we've seen, in recent decades many banks have effectively become two businesses in one: a "traditional" bank, taking in deposits and offering loans; and a much more risk-prone investment bank, dealing in securities. In many cases, such banks are now regarded as "too big to fail". This is not really a reflection on their size but more on their nature, and the risk that their collapse could lead to a systemic failure in the banking system (some people prefer their term "too complex to fail").

Are bankers overpaid?

When the chief executive of Royal Bank of Scotland, Stephen Hester, appeared before a parliamentary committee in London in early 2010, he had an embarrassing admission to make about his pay package (worth potentially about $15 million over three years): "If you ask my mother and father about my pay they'd say it was too high."

The compensation paid to bankers is one of the great running sores of the financial crisis. There's no doubt that it can be eye-popping – think of the estimated $100 million given to Charles Prince when he quit Citibank or the estimated $161 million for Stan O'Neal when he stepped down from Merrill Lynch. But what's more relevant in terms of financial regulation is not the absolute size of pay packages but how they're structured and how that shapes employees' behaviour.

Typically, fixed salary forms only a small part of a financial high-flyer's compensation; for examples, studies suggest that in 2006 it accounted for only about a quarter of CEO income in European banks and as little as 6% in the US. The rest usually comes in performance-based cash bonuses, stocks and stock options (which give the holder the right to buy shares in the future at a specified price).

How can these shape behaviour? Take bonuses. Typically, these are based on how well a bank has been doing over the past six or 12 months. As a result, they may encourage bankers to worry more about short-term profits than long-term stability. They can also encourage greater risk-taking. Think of a trader whose bonus is based on the profits he generates from his trades: there's no limit to the top end of his bonus, while the bottom end is limited to zero, in other words, no bonus and no deduction from his baseline salary. The bigger the profit he makes the bigger the bonus, but the penalty for a loss – no matter how big it is – remains at zero (although he may well lose his job). In this case, the trader wins if his gambles succeed, but it's the bank and its shareholders who pay if he racks up losses.

A number of approaches to restructuring executive compensation have been proposed. The details vary, but several ideas recur. For example, compensation shouldn't encourage employees to take risks that exceed the bank's overall risk appetite. It should also work in a way that lines up employees' interests with the longer-term concerns of shareholders. It should reflect the wider performance of the business, not just the individual's. And it should never reward employees in the short term for risks that may play out only over the long term.

> "A bank 'too big to fail' might be defined as referring to a bank that has grown in a manner that its failure would have systemic implications."
>
> *Financial Market Trends, Volume 2009, Issue 2*

This risk exists for two main reasons. First, banks generally rely on fairly small amounts of capital. For traditional banks this is usually tolerable; even during a downturn they can cover their losses (and if not, depositors are insured up to significant amounts in most countries, so a bank failure should not threaten the financial system as a whole). But, as we saw in the previous section, for investment-style banks, leveraging can greatly amplify losses. When these two different types of banks live under the same roof, losses on the investment side can threaten the traditional side. Second, trading in securities and derivatives typically enmeshes an investment bank in a vast web of obligations with other financial entities – banks, insurers, hedge funds and so on. Just as happened during the financial crisis, the failure of any one of these can send a chill throughout the entire system.

Let banks fail

If financial regulation is to become more effective, it needs to reduce moral hazard. In other words, banks and other financial institutions need to be allowed to fail – but without bringing down the entire banking system. A number of approaches have been proposed that might allow that to happen. For instance, systemically important banks might be required to produce a "living will" that would set out how they could be safely dismantled in the event of failure. Proponents argue this would force banks to clarify their legal structures and separate out their various activities. Another approach would involve legislation along the lines of the 1933 Glass-Steagall Act in the United States, which in effect created two classes of banks, commercial and investment. Its repeal in 1999 is seen by many as a contributing factor in the run-up to the financial crisis.

A proposal from the OECD calls for the operations of individual banks to be grouped under what's called a "non-operating holding company". This parent company would be able to raise capital in the stock market and invest it – transparently – in the bank's affiliates, which would be separate entities in legal terms. Because they would all be part of the same group, the affiliates could cut costs by sharing in areas like computing, technology systems and backroom operations. But their separateness would insulate each affiliate from a failure in the group. In the event of a crisis, the parent wouldn't be allowed to shift capital from one affiliate to the other – for instance from its commercial banking arm to its investment arm. If the investment arm failed, it could die without bringing down the entire bank. Such failures should become rarer in such a system, however. Separating out the bank's various capital pools means investors would know the real financial strength of each affiliate, and could thus make a more accurate risk assessment.

What's happening in financial regulation?

Around the world governments are pursuing various approaches to financial regulation: new and proposed rules and guidelines have also come from intergovernmental organisations such as the Bank for International Settlements and the Financial Stability Board, and from the OECD, which has produced a framework for financial regulation. The G20, too, has been active, and in 2009 agreed a series of pledges aimed at strengthening regulation. Some of these have been making their way into national legislation, for example the Dodd-Frank Act signed into law in the United States in July 2010.

There isn't the space here to explore all the proposals for reform in detail, but a few general themes have emerged:

➤ Improve transparency: banks' exposure to risk (both on and off their balance sheets) should be made much clearer, as should their relationship to offshore and special-purpose entities.

➤ Increase surveillance: central banks and other regulators should improve oversight of banks and financial institutions, ratings agencies and hedge funds, and develop better early warning systems.

➤ Revise capital and liquidity rules: banks should have a stronger capital base, and should have greater reserves of liquidity – *i.e.* resources that can be called on to meet short-term financing needs.

➤ Strengthen risk management and corporate governance: risk managers should be given more responsibility and greater influence over management. Directors should be knowledgeable and independent and should, as one OECD report suggests, maintain a "'healthy scepticism' in their assessment of the bank's strategies, policies and processes".

➤ Fix executive pay: bankers' compensation should encourage them to favour long-term growth and stability over riskier short-term profits.

➤ End "too big to fail": banks or parts of banks that fail need to be able to go out of business without damaging the entire financial system.

➤ Set global accounting standards: national and international agencies should set out rules for global, high-quality standards. Under such rules, bank capital, for example, would be defined and measured in the same way around the world, so increasing transparency.

This list just scratches the surface of what is being done and what needs to be done. For instance, it doesn't include proposals for a central "clearing house" for trades in derivative financial products, such as credit-default swaps, which would aim to increase transparency. Nor does it deal with how consumers could be protected in the financial maze: are specialised agencies needed, for example, and could improved financial education help people to better understand the risks and benefits of investments such as mortgages?

There's also a very important international element to financial regulation: after all, the biggest banks today are, almost by definition, global banks. This poses special challenges for national regulation, and underlines the usefulness of an international approach that's consistent and comprehensive. This would reduce the possibility of banks exploiting quirks and loopholes in national regulations to gain advantage. But it should also lead them to concentrate more resources on core business like deposit-taking and lending and to develop effective approaches to risk management and corporate governance.

What's being done to tackle tax evasion?

Mention tax havens and you may well think of some sunny island where taxes are non-existent and most companies are just a brass plate in a lawyer's office. Or, as *The Economist* puts it – with tongue only slightly in cheek – "a country or designated zone that has low or no taxes, or highly secretive banks, and often a warm climate and sandy beaches, which make it attractive to foreigners bent on tax avoidance or even tax evasion".

Whether these places will remain quite so attractive in the future is unclear. One of the side-effects of the crisis has been a fresh determination by governments to call time on tax evasion. At the G20 meeting in London in April 2009, leaders pledged "to take action against non-cooperative jurisdictions, including tax havens", and declared that "the era of banking secrecy is over".

In some ways this new willingness might seem surprising: while the role of tax havens in causing the crisis remains a matter for debate, their existence did at least facilitate banks' reckless appetite for risk. Equally, the existence of tax havens, and the problems they create, have been well known for many years. As far back as 1998, the OECD set out a definition of the characteristics of tax havens, and followed this two years later with a list of jurisdictions it judged fitted that bill.

But in recent years, a number of things have happened to make the position of tax havens increasingly untenable. In early 2008, police in Germany used data taken from a bank in Lichtenstein to investigate wealthy Germans suspected of using bank accounts in the tiny European principality to evade taxes. Chancellor Angela Merkel described the scale of the tax evasion as "beyond what I could have imagined". The United States Justice Department is also in the process of implementing an agreement with the Swiss bank UBS to turn over the names of almost 5,000 of its clients suspected of failing to pay US taxes.

Incidents such as these highlighted the need for tax administrations to be able to request information from each other in order to ensure taxes are paid. In the wake of the crisis, this has become an even bigger issue. Governments in many countries have run up big debts while trying to keep financial markets and the wider economy afloat. At the same time, declining economic activity has been eating into their tax take: falling demand means lower profits for companies, and thus lower corporate taxes, while rising unemployment means fewer workers to pay income taxes. That's another reason why governments are increasingly determined to ensure that the taxes they are owed are paid in full.

"At a time when governments around the world need tax revenues to address the global economic crisis, countering international tax evasion is more important than ever."

OECD's Current Tax Agenda

What are tax havens?

So, what exactly is a tax haven? For a historical perspective, it's interesting to look at the 1998 definition from the OECD, which set out four defining characteristics:

➤ No, or very low, taxes on income: in other words, income that would typically be taxed in most places – such as salaries, profits or earnings from rents – is not taxed or barely taxed.

➤ Insufficient exchange of information: authorities in other jurisdictions are unable to find out if their own citizens are stashing money in the haven.

➤ Lack of transparency: information on owners and other beneficiaries is not available or is not accessible.

➤ No substantial activities: a company or individual has a legal – but not a real – presence. For example, a sneaker manufacturer may be registered in the haven, but it's not making or distributing its sneakers from there.

Today, the emphasis has been put on exchange of information and transparency. Considering that many people probably think of tax havens solely in terms of low taxes, this might seem surprising. However, it's important to understand that it is the combination of no tax in a jurisdiction and the lack of exchange of information that allows tax evasion. If the country of residence were informed of assets or income held by its taxpayers in a tax haven, it would be in a position to tax them adequately So, if a jurisdiction levies no or low taxes on its own taxpayers, that's pretty much its own business. But if it admits funds from taxpayers in another jurisdiction, and refuses to respond to requests for information about those funds, then it becomes everyone's business.

And everyone really does mean *everyone*: the work that governments do – from building roads to providing healthcare – is paid for by taxpayers. When individuals and businesses are able to evade paying the taxes they are legally required to pay, it means higher tax bills for everyone else. In poorer countries, the cost of tax evasion is even starker, and can be measured in terms of lack of basic infrastructure such as schools and hospitals and lost lives. According to some estimates, developing countries lose to tax havens three times what they get in aid from developed countries. "If taxes on assets hidden by tax dodgers were collected in their owners' jurisdictions," says OECD Secretary-General Angel Gurría, "billions of dollars could become available for financing development."

What has changed?

G20 leaders have said they're determined to act on tax evasion, but what's changed in reality? Perhaps the biggest change is the number of jurisdictions that are now making and implementing commitments to exchange information with other jurisdictions under a global standard developed by the OECD. Much of this has happened through the OECD Global Forum on Transparency and Exchange of Information, a body linked to the OECD but with a much broader membership – more than 90 jurisdictions (as of mid-2010), including pretty much all the world's major financial centres.

What does exchange of information involve? Crucially, tax jurisdictions must ensure they collect reliable and relevant information, and make it available when asked to. They also cannot invoke their own bank secrecy laws or domestic tax interests as a defence for turning down such requests.

What it *doesn't* involve is automatic release of information. Some critics have suggested it should, but such an approach has real problems. For one thing, it would generate huge amounts of data, which many jurisdictions would struggle to manage. Some countries, on a voluntary basis, are involved in automatic exchange and draw benefits from it. However, while the OECD standard allows for automatic exchange of information it doesn't make it compulsory.

The standard also includes a high level of protection of taxpayers' rights, including the right to confidentiality. Jurisdictions seeking information also won't be able to launch "fishing expeditions" – demanding huge swathes of information in the hope that some of it might be useful – but will only be able to request information that's "foreseeably relevant".

To be a member of the Global Forum, jurisdictions must commit to internationally agreed tax standards, which include activities like exchange of information, and to "peer review", a process that began early in 2010 and that requires jurisdictions to open themselves up to inspection by other members of the Global Forum. All members of the Global Forum – both OECD and non-OECD economies – will undergo a peer review. Failure to pass the test could leave them open to sanctions from other governments or group of countries (neither the Global Forum nor the OECD has the authority to impose penalties).

But the threat of sanctions is likely to be outweighed by the sheer momentum for reform that has built up over the past few years, says Andrew Auerbach, an OECD tax expert. "It used to be that transparency was seen as a competitive disadvantage," he says. "Now it's seen as an advantage. Jurisdictions want to be seen to – and to actually adhere to – the standards because competitively it's seen as disastrous not to. Because the G20 is focusing on this and wants actions, businesses and individuals are saying, 'You know, if I'm in that place that's not adhering to the standards, I'm just asking for trouble'."

Black, white and grey ...

Throughout 2009, there was much talk in the media of OECD tax "blacklists", "greylists" and even "whitelists". While never formally endorsed, these terms did reflect a process, whereby the OECD issued "progress reports" naming jurisdictions that were seen as not having made sufficient commitments to the necessary standards. The process is complicated, but in simple terms a test was set that required jurisdictions to show their commitment to the international agreement on exchanging tax information by agreeing to a minimum number of exchange-of-information agreements with other jurisdictions. There has been some criticism of this process, with allegations that some tax havens are accumulating the required number of agreements by simply signing deals with other havens. However, this was only a first stage: the peer-review process will now become the real test of whether jurisdictions are living up to their commitments.

Can we agree on global ethical standards?

The crisis has thrown up many questions, not the least of which concerns the "values" of the global economy. "In our view," Angela Merkel and Jan Peter Balkenende wrote in 2009, "it is … indispensable that market forces are not only checked through regulations and oversight, but also by a robust global framework of common values that sets clear limits to excessive and irresponsible action."

Chancellor Merkel's stance on these issues is worth noting: she has been a determined advocate of a "Global Charter for Sustainable Economic Activity" – an idea aimed at promoting a better balance between market forces and the societies they serve, so ensuring a "stable, socially balanced and sustainable development of the global economy".

The proposed Charter would cover a wide range of issues, including economic stability, employment and social policies, and the environment. The aim would be to build an international consensus behind "a collection of overarching principles linking economic liberty with accountability and responsibility as the basic cornerstones of economic activity". These ideas have also been echoed by the G20, which in September 2009 adopted "Core Values for Sustainable Economic Activity" including "those of propriety, integrity, and transparency".

The Lecce Framework

The final shape of any Global Charter remains to be seen, but it's likely to include a number of different strands. One of these may be the so-called "Lecce Framework", a set of guidelines and frameworks drawing on existing agreements created by bodies like the OECD. These sorts of agreements are often referred to as "soft law", which means they don't carry fixed sanctions, such as fines and penalties, but are instead "policed" by processes such as peer review, where governments examine each other's performance in specific areas. In some cases, soft law can become "hard", as when a country uses international guidelines as the basis for creating binding legislation or regulations.

What does soft law cover? In addition to tax evasion, which was discussed in the previous section, here are a couple of examples of areas that some OECD guidelines and agreements address:

Bribery and corruption: Few forces are more corrosive in societies and economies than bribery and corruption. They destroy people's trust in leaders, distort competition and push resources into the wrong areas – for instance, corrupt officials may favour big-ticket projects like dams and power stations, which offer a greater potential for kickbacks, rather than more useful projects like schools and hospitals.

A number of international agreements seek to tackle these issues, including the United Nations Convention against Corruption and the OECD Anti-Bribery Convention. Some OECD soft laws have gone on to become hard law – for example, a recommendation in the mid-1990s that bribes paid to foreign officials should not be tax-deductible is now embedded in the tax laws of many countries.

Business behaviour: As we saw earlier in this chapter, the crisis helped expose some serious shortcomings in corporate governance, with procedures often failing to safeguard against excessive risk taking in financial companies.

> "When they were put to a test, corporate governance routines did not serve their purpose to safeguard against excessive risk taking in a number of financial services companies...."
>
> Grant Kirkpatrick, *OECD Financial Market Trends* (2009)

To work effectively, corporate governance needs to deal with both the rights *and* the responsibilities of a company's management, its board, shareholders, employees, clients and others. Structures, responsibilities and procedures need to be clearly set out, and information needs to be disclosed in a way that's timely, accurate and transparent. These issues are addressed in a number of OECD agreements, including the OECD Principles of Corporate Governance and the OECD Guidelines for Multinational Enterprises.

Building bricks

Revised versions of such agreements may well form the "bricks" of the more overarching approach championed by Chancellor Merkel and other leaders. Just as the crisis revealed failures in how banks and businesses operate, it also highlighted areas in regulation – from legally binding rules to soft law – that need to be updated. That process will form a key task in designing a Lecce Framework.

That's likely to be a challenging process. Quite simply, governments don't always see eye to eye on how best to regulate the global economy, whether through binding laws or soft law. Anglophone countries, such as the United States and United Kingdom, have tended to favour a lighter regulatory hand; continental European countries, such as Germany and France, have often leaned towards a more hands-on approach. Equally, some countries are uncomfortable with the idea of subjecting lucrative industries like financial services to international regulations that they fear could limit their ability to compete globally.

Carrots or sticks?

There is also the question of whether frameworks and guidelines that are not accompanied by real sanctions have sufficient "teeth" to be effective. Individual countries tend to regard national sovereignty as paramount in most areas, so governments are usually slow to sign up for legally binding agreements. The result, as we've seen, is that global governance often takes the form of soft law.

Such approaches have benefits and drawbacks. On the one hand, where there are no real sanctions, especially on businesses, there may be a risk that global standards exist in name only. "Most [intergovernmental organisations] are designed to discipline signatory governments by moral suasion or in some cases, sanctions, but not corporations which remain completely unregulated at the global level," Kimon Valaskakis, a former Canadian ambassador to the OECD and president of the New School of Athens, has argued. "As a result, the 'guidelines' and 'frameworks' end up having the same status as New Year Resolutions, such as quitting smoking or losing weight. Most of them are just not kept."

On the other hand, as OECD Secretary-General Angel Gurría has pointed out, processes without sanctions "are easier to join. People don't need to dot every 'i' and cross every 't' if they aren't worried about getting whacked by sanctions." Clearly, the more governments and businesses that sign up to international agreements, the greater the potential for setting global standards.

Sanctions – the "stick" in the carrot and stick – are not the only way to change behaviour. Incentives can be effective, too. For example, countries that sign non-binding international agreements may receive more favourable treatment in areas like trade and investment from other signatories. At the corporate level, too, incentives – "carrots" – can play an important role in shaping behaviour. For instance, tax systems can make it more attractive for managers to receive bonuses in the form of long-term stock holdings rather than in cash, which may steer them towards seeking long-term profitability rather than quick returns.

Questioning the future

The crisis has revealed shortcomings in our understanding of the global economy. That's why there's been so much talk about the need for new rules and regulations. But, in its own way, the crisis has also helped to change the global economy, adding hugely to many countries' national debt, for instance. In some ways, nothing will ever be quite the same again. So what will be the long-term impact of the crisis? In the next, and last, chapter of this book, we look at some of the ways in which the crisis will continue to shape the global economy and how we think about it.

Find Out More

OECD

On the Internet

For an introduction to OECD work on **financial markets**, go to *www.oecd.org/finance*; for **corporate governance**, click on *www.oecd.org/daf* and then on the link for "Lessons from the Financial Crisis"; for the OECD Principals on Corporate Governance, go to *www.oecd.org/daf/corporate/principles*.

To find out about OECD work on **taxation** and **tax policy**, go to *www.oecd.org/taxation*, and click on the link for "The OECD's Current Tax Agenda". For the **Global Forum on Transparency and Exchange of Information for Tax Purposes**, go to *www.oecd.org/tax/transparency*.

To find out about OECD work on **bribery** and **corruption**, go to *www.oecd.org/corruption*.

For an introduction to OECD work on creating the "**Global Standard**", go to *www.oecd.org/globalstandard*; add "/blog" to get to the Global Standard blog.

Publications

The Financial Crisis: Reform and Exit Strategies (2009): Among the topics covered in this book is the reform of financial governance with the aim of ensuring a healthier balance between risk and reward and restoring public confidence in financial markets.

Financial Market Trends (journal): A number of articles may be of special interest, including "The Corporate Governance Lessons from the Financial Crisis" (Vol. 2009, No. 1), and "The Elephant in the Room: The Need to Deal with What Banks Do" (Vol. 2009, No. 2).

Tax Co-operation – Towards a Level Playing Field: An annual review of the legal and administrative frameworks for transparency and exchange of information for tax purposes in OECD and non-OECD Countries. The most recent edition covers 87 countries.

... AND OTHER SOURCES

IMF – Reforming the International Financial System: A special section on the International Monetary Fund's website that brings together information about the continuing efforts to reform the international financial system. *www.imf.org/external/NP/EXR/key/quotav.htm*

Financial Stability Forum (*www.financialstabilityboard.org*): Created as a response to the crisis (but as a successor to the Financial Stability Board), the Forum's role is to coordinate the work of national financial authorities and international standard-setting bodies and to develop and promote the implementation of effective regulatory, supervisory and other financial sector policies.

Bank for International Settlements (*www.bis.org*): Sometimes dubbed "the central banks' central bank", the BIS has a number of roles, including serving as a forum for debate and discussion, carrying out monetary and economic research, and setting standards in areas such as capital requirements.

7

Regardless of the pace of recovery, the recession will have long-term economic and social consequences, some of which may not become fully apparent for years to come. To think about some of these long-term impacts, this chapter poses five questions for the future.

The Future: Five Questions

By way of introduction ...

Perhaps no image from the Great Depression of the 1930s is more iconic than "Migrant Mother", a photograph by Dorothea Lange. It shows a tired-looking woman staring out from under a rough canvas tent; in her arms a baby is nestling, against her shoulders two older children are resting.

The woman's name was Florence Owens Thompson, and she was travelling with her family through California looking for work when she was spotted by Lange. "I saw and approached the hungry and desperate mother, as if drawn by a magnet," the photographer later recalled. "I did not ask her name or her history. She told me her age, that she was 32. She said that they had been living on frozen vegetables from the surrounding fields, and birds that the children killed."

Eighty years on, it's hard to think of a single image that bears such eloquent witness to our era's "Great Recession". That's not too surprising. Even though many people have lost their jobs, and some their homes, the suffering and hardship of the 1930s have not been repeated. Indeed, as economies continue their slow recovery, it's tempting to imagine that this slowdown will soon be forgotten – just a blip in the world's otherwise orderly economic progression.

▶ Tempting, but dangerous. Just as the Great Depression defined the lives of a generation and reshaped the world's economic and political contours, the recession we've lived through will have long-term consequences. Some of these will be economic, some social, and some may not become fully apparent for years to come. To think about some of these long-term impacts, this chapter poses five questions:

➤ What's the long-term economic impact?

➤ When will government policy get back to normal?

➤ Has the global balance shifted?

➤ Can the crisis become a green opportunity?

➤ And, does economics need a rethink?

What's the long-term economic impact?

"Annual income £20, annual expenditure £19 19s 6d, result happiness," declares Mr. Micawber in Dickens' *David Copperfield*. "Annual income £20, annual expenditure £20 0s 6d, result misery. The blossom is blighted, the leaf is withered, the God of day goes down upon the dreary scene, and – and in short you are forever floored."

"Floored" might be a little strong but, thanks to the actions they took during the crisis, many governments are now hunched rather lower under the weight of debt and deficits. (Remember, in very basic terms, a deficit occurs when a government spends more than it earns in a given year; a debt is the accumulation of such deficits over time.) This legacy is likely to hang around for some time, and it will shape the course of governments' future spending, including their ability to cope with social and economic change, such as population ageing.

The price of borrowing

In OECD countries, the national debt has risen during the crisis by about 30 percentage points and is now typically approaching 100% of GDP. In other words, countries' borrowings are now equivalent to their entire economic output. Deficits – which are more closely watched than debts – have also deteriorated. In 2000, OECD governments were actually earning a little more than they were spending; by 2009, average annual borrowings were equivalent to about 8% of GDP. Most economists believe these increased burdens are justified – after all, if governments hadn't acted so swiftly we might now be in the midst of the Second Great Depression.

Indeed, despite Mr. Micawber's warnings, debt in itself isn't a bad thing, either for governments or individuals – think of all those people with long-term student loans or mortgages. The problems really begin if your lenders start to wonder if you can pay back your borrowings. For some countries that has become quite an issue.

Typically, governments borrow money by auctioning bonds on the international money markets. In the fast-moving, high-flying world of finance, these can look a little dull: they take a long time to mature – often decades – and the interest rates are usually fairly low. But they are very secure – they're backed by the government of a country, after all, which makes them attractive. That lure diminishes, however, if bond buyers are worried about the risk of a "sovereign debt default" –

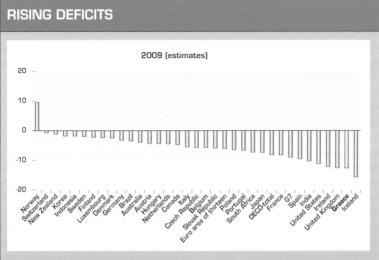

RISING DEFICITS

2009 (estimates)

Government deficits – in basic terms, governments' spending minus their earnings – have risen sharply during the crisis. In a number of countries in the euro zone, they now exceed the 3% limit set down in the rules that established the single European currency. In Greece, for example, the deficit is above 12% of GDP. The deteriorating state of public finances has raised fears that some governments may not be able to meet their debts, which has increased the cost of their borrowing.

Source: OECD Economic Outlook.

StatLink ⬛ᵍᵖ *http://dx.doi.org/10.1787/888932320656*

in other words, will this government be able to pay its debts when the time comes?

One way in which these doubts are reflected is in interest rates on government bonds – if buyers have doubts about a country's economic prospects they'll want a higher return. According to data compiled by *The Wall Street Journal*, in March 2007 – before the crisis struck – Greece was paying an interest rate on its bonds that was about a quarter of a percentage point higher than the German rate. Three years later, in March 2010, following sharp increases in the Greek government's borrowing, the Greek premium had risen to 3.25 percentage points (and it would later rise higher still). This meant Greece now had to pay higher interest rates to borrow money, which, in turn, only added to its borrowing needs.

OECD Insights: From Crisis to Recovery

So, it's important for governments to be able to reassure the markets that they can go on paying their debts. That doesn't mean cutting the size of them straight away. As we'll see later in this chapter, the recoveries in some countries are still relatively weak and special measures to support economies will be needed for some time yet. But to keep the confidence of the markets, governments do need to show they recognise the debt problem and signal how they ultimately plan to deal with it.

Ways to cut deficits

Boil it down, and governments really have only two options when it comes to cutting deficits – raise taxes or cut spending.

Raise taxes: Rarely popular with the voters, tax rises mean more income for governments and, thus, reduced borrowing needs. But, aside from the political obstacles, there are limits to how far most governments feel they can go (although people in different countries vary greatly in their appetites for tax). If taxes rise too high they reduce consumers' spending power as well as businesses' incentives and capacity to invest. In a globalised economy, they may also lead individuals and companies to relocate to lower-tax countries.

That said, there's a lot of room for manoeuvre in taxation, and some tax rises may be less painful than others. For instance, property taxes and indirect taxes, such as sales and value-added taxes, seem to have less of an impact on economic activity than income taxes. And "green" taxes could deliver the twin benefits of boosting government coffers while discouraging carbon emissions.

Cut spending: Once governments start spending in an area, it can be hard for them to stop. Any group that's benefiting from spending may feel a cut very sharply, and may be motivated to protest loudly. By contrast, the benefits from a cut may be spread out so widely across society (*e.g.* to taxpayers in general), it can be hard for anyone to feel sufficiently motivated to come out in support.

In addition to such political challenges, there are important issues of economic strategy that need to be considered when cutting spending. For example, education eats up a large slice of public spending in OECD countries – about 13% – but much of that can be thought of as an investment in human capital that will pay off in long-term economic growth. Similarly, spending on innovation and R&D can seem expensive in the short run, but can help drive growth for years to come. Decisions on spending can also be made that will have little immediate impact, making them more politically acceptable, but that have the potential to bring long-term returns, such as changes to pensions and healthcare provision.

The growth solution

There is a third, highly attractive, solution we haven't mentioned – governments can grow their way out of debt. (Some academic economists talk about a fourth approach in which governments "inflate" their way out of debt by triggering a short, sharp burst of inflation. In practice, this would be difficult to engineer.) When an economy is growing, governments automatically spend less on welfare as unemployment falls and earn more from taxes as wages rise and company profits strengthen. The problem is that, unlike the first two options – tax rises and spending cuts – governments can't simply make it happen. They can, however, create circumstances through the right mix of taxation and investment that make growth more likely.

> **"Past experience with financial crises indicates that GDP and income levels are unlikely to return any time soon to their initially projected path."**
>
> *Economic Policy Reforms 2010: Going for Growth*

Unfortunately, the foundations for building that growth are not as strong as they once were. One reason for this lies in the lingering impact of the recession. Economists often think of economies in terms of their potential output – in effect, this is the total GDP that could be produced over the long term if everyone who wanted to work had a job and every factory was working at full steam, and so on.

In the wake of the crisis, the potential economic output of OECD countries is forecast to be 3% lower than it would have been if they hadn't been hit by the recession. For some countries, the impact will be much greater – about 4% for Italy, just under 11% for Spain and a little under 12% for Ireland. Why? There are two main reasons: first, the pre-crisis appetite for risk has faded, which will make things like borrowing capital for investment more expensive, so companies will find it harder to expand; second, unemployment is likely to remain high, which in itself dampens economic activity.

What about growth rates – *i.e.* the amount by which an economy expands each year? In theory, OECD economies could return quite swiftly to their average annual pre-crisis growth rates of about 2% to 2.25% (albeit from a lower base than before). In practice, growth in developed countries faces some serious obstacles and is forecast to hover around 1.75% over the long term. The main reason for this lies less in the legacy of the recession and more in a problem that's been brewing for many years – ageing populations.

Fairness between the generations

In much of the OECD area, the population is getting steadily older as fewer babies are born and more people live to a grand old age. In OECD countries in 2000, there were about 27 people of retirement age for every 100 active workers. By 2050, that ratio is forecast to rise to about 62 retirees for every 100 workers. And in some countries, such as Spain, Japan, Korea and Japan, it's forecast to be more than 90. Even with higher retirement ages the size of the workforce looks set to fall, which means fewer workers to support an ever-growing slice of the population.

These are not new issues, but the crisis has thrown them into even sharper relief. In part this reflects a perception that the "baby boomers" (sometimes defined as people born between 1946 and 1964) will enjoy all the benefits of a strong social welfare system but will hand on huge national debts to their children and grandchildren. One British writer, 29-year-old Andrew Hankinson, puts it this way: "No doubt the older generation will have a good time with their free bus passes and villas in Spain. They'll enjoy the pensions and property... . We're just cheap labour, here to fund a bit more wealth. We know that now. And don't worry, we'll pay off the debt." For the sake of fairness, if nothing else, the bill for fighting one generation's crisis can't simply be presented for payment to the next generation.

As we saw in Chapter 5, it's also important to start planning now to cope with the shifting age balance in our societies – otherwise, the rise in debt during the crisis could look very minor compared with what's to come. According to economists at the Bank for International Settlements, if governments stick to their current spending commitments on pensions and the like, national debt in some OECD countries could hit more than 400% of GDP by 2040. In reality, that could never happen – financial markets would stop lending to a country long before its borrowing hit such heights. But the forecast is a warning about the scale of this looming challenge. The loss of economic output during the recession won't make solving it any easier, but it may engender a new sense of economic reality about the need to start acting now.

When will government policy get back to normal?

In the immediate post-crisis era, commentators often liked using medical metaphors – economies were "out of intensive care but still on life support" or, better still, "walking on crutches". The point they were making was that, yes, there was economic recovery but it wasn't yet fully self-sustaining.

Especially in developed countries, like those in the OECD area, the initial phases of recovery were driven by policy decisions – low interest rates, tax cuts, extra spending on infrastructure – rather than consumer and business activity. By contrast, recovery in many developing and emerging countries was more organic (although in some, notably China, government intervention is also providing a major stimulus).

The slowness of the return to economic normality is not too surprising: financial crises cast long shadows. The shock to the confidence of businesses and consumers, and to their balance sheets, can take years to heal, robbing economies of the usual post-recession stimulants, such as consumer demand that's built up during a downturn.

So, to avoid a spiral into an economic depression, governments have had to go on providing extraordinary – perhaps unprecedented – support to the economy. But there's a limit to how long this can continue. For one thing, it's expensive: as we saw in the previous section, government's annual deficits have risen sharply. That can't go on forever. Policy interventions can also lead to unwelcome dynamics in economies. For example, ultra-low interest rates may make borrowing relatively cheap – which can stimulate the economy – but they also risk fuelling new bubbles in asset prices similar to those that led up to the crisis.

And there's the problem of what to do if there's another downturn. With interest rates already at such low levels, there's little room for manoeuvre in sending them lower. If another recession hit, that means governments would be robbed of one of their chief economic weapons.

Timing is everything …

At some stage, then, government policy is going to have to return to normal. But, as with so much else in life, timing is everything. Move too fast, and nascent recoveries could be strangled at birth; wait too long, and the debt burden will go on growing. Indeed, this question of when and how to start cutting back has sparked intense debate. For example, the Nobel laureate Paul Krugman has criticised what he sees as premature efforts to withdraw support from still-weak economies, saying the "idea that what depressed economies really need is even more suffering seems to be the new conventional wisdom". By contrast, OECD Chief Economist Pier Carlo Padoan has argued that Europe's sovereign debt problems are a warning that the risks in the global economy have shifted. In this unsettled financial environment, governments need to get out ahead of markets or risk becoming hostage to them. "We are not arguing for contractionary policy, but for progressively less stimulus," Padoan has said. "In fact, stimulus should not be withdrawn completely until the economy returns to full employment. But the process should be started fairly soon, to take into account the well known long and variable monetary policy lags."

Even though many governments have already begun the process of winding down stimulus measures, a full return to normality will take some time yet and is likely to happen at a varying pace across different sectors of the economy. For example, in some countries, the effective "nationalisations" of some banks and financial institutions may take many years to unwind. Even more modest steps, such as measures to recapitalise banks, will take time and will probably not fully come to an end until there's full implementation of financial-market reforms. By contrast, other support, such as "cash for clunker" schemes to support the automotive industry, have already ended in many countries.

"Fiscal consolidation must be designed and implemented to support growth …"

Pier Carlo Padoan, *OECD Economic Outlook Vol. 2010/1*

But even if it takes years to fully unwind their various interventions, governments need to set out roadmaps for how they're going to do this to retain the confidence of international lenders. There are other issues, too. In the shorter term, cutbacks shouldn't undermine attempts to get unemployed people back to work. Over the longer term, the sort of government spending that helps lay foundations for future growth – such as investment in education, training and research and development – needs to remain a priority, even if that means finding ways to do more with less.

Has the global balance shifted?

An enduring image from the early days of the crisis was the emergency summit of leaders in Washington, DC, in November 2008. Presided over by then-US President George W. Bush, it brought together the likes of France's Nicolas Sarkozy, Germany's Angela Merkel and Japan's Taro Aso. But there was another group of leaders there, too – India's Manmohan Singh, China's Hu Jintao, Brazil's Lula da Silva and others.

For many observers, the substance of those Washington discussions was less important than the fact they happened at all: this was the first time that heads of government from the world's leading and emerging economies had met under the G20 umbrella. The timing – just as the full scale of the financial crisis was becoming apparent – seemed to send a clear signal that the crisis was global and needed a global response. But that couldn't just come from the traditional G8 economic powerhouses. From now on, a much wider group of developed and emerging economies would need to play a role in such gatherings.

The crisis didn't cause this shift in the balance of global economic power. Indeed, if anything, it was the other way around. "The origins of the crisis lay in our inability to cope with the consequences of the entry into the world trading system of countries such as China, India, and the former Soviet empire – in a word, globalisation," the governor of the Bank of England, Mervyn King, has stated. The numbers back this up. In 1980, high-income countries (typically, those found in the OECD area plus some others) accounted for 71% of the global economy. By 2008, that had fallen to 56%, thanks in large part to the emergence of countries like China and India. As emerging economies have recovered more strongly from the crisis than many developed economies, that share is unlikely to stop growing.

But it wasn't simply the emergence of transition countries over the past couple of decades that led to the crisis. As we saw in Chapter 2, the phenomenon was also accompanied by growing imbalances in the world economy. In simple terms, manufacturers in transition economies sold vast amounts of goods to Western consumers, and then, rather than spending the earnings, saved them by buying the likes of US Treasury bonds. Or, as Mervyn King has said, "The benefits in terms of trade were visible; the costs of the implied capital flows were not."

What are coupling and decoupling?

If the US sneezes, does the rest of the world catch cold? That's the question at the heart of the great **coupling** vs. **decoupling** debate. Over the years there have been several shifts in opinion. At one time, it seemed that the economies of China and other developing countries were growing independently of what was happening in developed economies. Then the global recession came along, appearing to indicate that the economies of the world were coupled. But the rapid pace of recovery in transition economies compared to those in the OECD area has reawakened interest in decoupling. If the idea is borne out, it could add a brand new dynamic to the global economy.

Clearly, such imbalances could not continue forever. To some extent, the subsequent recession has smoothed out these imbalances – for instance, Western consumers cut back on their spending. But as the world economy recovers, there's concern that too little has been done to deal with them over the longer term. There is a wide range of possible solutions, and some of them offer the prospect of a valuable double dividend. For instance, the OECD has called on China to save less and spend more in areas like pensions, health and education. This would help to address both social inequalities in China and broader global imbalances. There has also been pressure on China to allow greater flexibility in the exchange rate of its currency, the yuan, so that it better reflects the country's trading strength.

> "While, like many other countries China needs to foster social cohesion, unlike many other countries, yours is in the enviable position of having the fiscal room to do it."
>
> Angel Gurría, speech to the China Development Forum, Beijing, March 2010

There's no point pretending that finding the answers to these global imbalances will be easy. In the post-crisis era, they are likely to be a source of continuing economic and political tensions. But, equally, it would be very wrong to view these issues, and the wider shifts in the global economy, as zero-sum games – *i.e.* where one person's gains are another's losses. Already, the economic emergence of countries like China, India and Brazil has transformed the lives of millions of people for the better. It has created new engines for the global economy and for development in some of the world's poorest countries. The challenge in the years to come will be to create new ways of overseeing the global economy that take account of the changed landscape while maximising the benefits for all.

Can the crisis be a green opportunity?

While much of the world's attention has been focused on fighting the impact of the financial crisis, another even more profound problem continues to simmer – climate change. The potential costs of climate change are regularly and widely discussed – rising sea levels, loss of biodiversity, spread of human disease and so on. Equally, the costs of fighting climate change are widely bandied about: for example, the UNFCCC, a United Nations agency that works on climate change issues, has estimated that by 2030 developing countries will need inflows equal to tens of billions of dollars a year, and perhaps more than $100 billion a year, if they are to adapt to changing climate.

What's less widely understood, however, is the idea that investing in environmentally friendly technologies and approaches could deliver a double dividend – a cleaner environment *and* economic growth.

> **"We are convinced that the conversion of our economies into low carbon economies can be an important source of growth and employment."**
>
> Angel Gurría, speech in Seoul, November 2009

The recession has provided a rare opportunity to make such investments, for two reasons. First, because of reduced economic activity, the "opportunity cost" is lower – essentially, the reduction of overall business activity has reduced competing opportunities for investment. Second, as governments have to spend more to boost economic activity anyway, they may as well do some of it in a more eco-friendly way. In a number of countries, a sizeable chunk of this money has gone to "green" or "greenish" projects, for example, renewable energy and railways. ("Cash for clunker" programmes have more mixed environmental benefits: it's true that newer models tend to be more fuel efficient, but there's an environmental cost to building them and taking older cars off the roads before the end of their useful lives.) Korea announced investment of about $40 billion in a "Green New Deal" with the aim of creating 960 000 jobs in areas like renewable energy, energy efficiency and transport, while France spent just over a fifth of its $33 billion stimulus packages in similar ways. And China devoted about 40% of its $586 billion stimulus package to green projects, including support for wind and solar power, which has helped to turn the country into the world's biggest market for renewables.

Such measures are impressive, but it's important to analyse seriously their effectiveness and to ensure that public funds yield maximum impact. Critics have argued that this is not always the case. For instance, Citigroup estimated that in 2009, about 30% of China's wind-power assets were not in use, in large part because wind farms were not connected to the grid. In Germany, an independent research institute claimed that the government's approach to supporting the country's extensive renewable energy sector had resulted in "… massive expenditures that show little long-term promise for stimulating the economy, protecting the environment, or increasing energy security". To make the most of the crisis as a "green" opportunity, policies will need to be carefully thought out to ensure that investment in green growth yields both economic and environment benefits.

What is the Green Growth Strategy?

In 2009, the OECD began work on a **Green Growth Strategy** with the aim of charting a course towards economies that produce growth based on lower carbon emissions. Just as with research and development, which are being studied in the OECD's Innovation Strategy, going green can help drive long-term economic growth, through, for example, investments in renewable energy and improved efficiency in the use of energy and materials. The Green Growth Strategy is analysing the impact and interaction of economic and environmental policies together, examining ways to spur eco-innovation and thinking about other key issues related to a transition to a greener economy, such as jobs and skills, investment, taxation, trade and development.

Does economics need a rethink?

In November 2008, when the world seemed on the brink of financial collapse, an elderly British lady wondered aloud about the origins of the crisis: "Why did nobody notice it?" she asked. Her words might have gone unnoticed except for one thing: she was Queen Elizabeth II and she was speaking during a visit to the world-renowned London School of Economics.

In truth, it's not fair to say that *nobody* saw it coming. As early as September 2006, according to *The New York Times*, the academic and commentator Nouriel Roubini warned a gathering of IMF economists that a huge crisis was brewing, one that would see "homeowners defaulting on mortgages, trillions of dollars of mortgage-backed securities unravelling worldwide and the global financial system shuddering to a halt". Few could rival that for an overview of the looming catastrophe. But there were also warnings about particular problems in the run-up to the crisis – global imbalances, the housing bubble, the risk posed by laxly regulated financial products.

Unfortunately, too few people put all these pieces of the jigsaw together to create a complete picture of the looming crisis. In the words of a letter written by British economists in response to the Queen's question, "The failure to foresee the timing, extent and severity of the crisis and to head it off … was principally a failure of the collective imagination of many bright people … to understand the risks to the system as a whole."

Why was there such a failure? Was it because economists simply failed to pick up the signals in this particular situation? Or was it something bigger – a failure in how economists generally understand the world and the economy? Not surprisingly, the crisis has led to soul searching in the profession: according to US economist and Nobel laureate Paul Krugman, over the past three decades macroeconomics – *i.e.* "big picture" economics – was "spectacularly useless at best, and positively harmful at worst". While that probably represents an extreme view, it does reflect a growing tendency to question some ideas that have gained dominance in macroeconomics since the early 1970s.

Two ideas have come under particular fire. The first is the "efficient markets hypothesis". In very basic terms, this states that markets will always settle on prices for financial assets like stocks and bonds that are "right" – by necessity prices "reflect everything that is known about economic fundamentals, such as inflation, exports, and corporate profitability", as John Cassidy has written. If prices rise above levels justified by economic fundamentals, someone will step in and sell; if they fall below, someone will spot the opportunity and buy. The second is the "rational expectations hypothesis". Again, in very simple terms, this suggests that when it comes to thinking about the future, people have "rational" expectations and behave accordingly. Assuming they're working from the same information, people will develop a collective sense of where inflation and interest rates are heading, which will guide their decisions.

Personal view: where now?

Some thoughts on the future of economics from William R. White, former chief economist at the Bank for International Settlements (BIS) and now chair of the OECD's Economic and Development Review Committee.

How big an impact has the crisis had on macroeconomics?

I was at a conference organized by George Soros. Just about any big name you can think of was there – Jeff Sachs, Ken Rogoff, George Akerlof, Joe Stiglitz. They were there supporting the idea that we need new economic thinking. I took a lot of solace from that because, whatever profession you're in, peer review is a very big thing. If you're in the second rank of academic thinkers, you don't have any choice but to go along with what the other people say is important: "This is the way we do economics." It's only the top rank people who can say, "No I think this is not true, and I'm prepared to say so."

What needs rethinking in economics?

There's a lot of stuff that isn't there – financial institutions, feedback effects. All of this stuff is very, very hard. I don't want to disparage current modelling, but the fact of the matter is it's all very hard. But I do think progress is being made – something has started.

Even before the crisis, there had been growing interest in ideas like behavioural economics ....

That's right. You have ideas like fractal economics and economics as biology – thinking of economies as living systems, in which you have elements competing for scarce resources, and then adapting, and then other elements adapting in response. It's just a different way of looking at these things. The problem with classical mechanics is that everything stays the same – it sees economies as being closer to a machine than an organism. Things change, and models don't always get that.

Has economics been too sure of itself?

When I give talks, I very often start off with an epistemological introduction – how do we know we know? I like Mark Twain's quote – "It ain't what you don't know that gets you into trouble. It's what you know for sure that just ain't so." We've been assuming that we understand what's going on ....

How should this be reflected in the real world?

My attitude has always been that, given how little we know, instead of following a maximizing strategy for economic growth, we should follow a kind-of "mini-maxing" strategy – make sure we're not building up risks that are going to come back and cause us enormous problems.

It's hard to overstate the influence ideas like these have had in how economies are thought of and in how governments regulate them. By and large, they have tended to foster a strong belief that financial markets are best left to themselves, encouraging a "hands-off" approach to regulation. However, the scale of the boom and bust in property prices and the huge problems created by unregulated financial products has cast doubt on whether these hypotheses can really be said to reflect reality.

Other approaches, too, have come in for criticism. For example, the financial sector traditionally hasn't featured prominently when economists formally think of the economy. In economic models, banks and financial market are often treated as a "given" – basically, intermediaries between economic agents like companies and investors, but not really having an impact in their own right. Again, the impact of the crisis may change such mindsets.

So, these are challenging times for economists. But that's not necessarily a bad thing. "Academics, to be quite frank, sniff an opportunity here – new research, new ideas, new papers," says Professor Tim Besley of the LSE, who was one of the co-authors of that letter to the Queen. "That said, there are some economists who think this critique of economists has been overplayed," he adds. "But in academic circles, there's a mass of opportunity to investigate new issues and to think about old issues in a new way…."

By way of conclusion …

Until 1697, all swans were white. If you lived in Europe, the idea that a swan might not be white was an impossibility, something only a crazy person would think. And then, in that year, a group of Dutch explorers in Australia found the impossible: black swans.

The black swan has become one of the enduring images of the crisis, thanks in large part to the book of the same title written by the academic and former trader Nassim Nicholas Taleb and published on the eve of the crisis in 2007. Taleb argues that a "Black Swan Event" has three characteristics: it is totally unexpected and impossible to predict from past events; it has major consequences; and it is something humans attempt to explain away in retrospect – "we knew it was coming all along".

For most of us, the crisis we've just lived through was a Black Swan Event: we didn't see it coming; it will continue to shape our economies for years to come; and, at some level, we may be in danger now of beginning to rationalize it retrospectively – "it was just another recession, these things happen". To do so would be foolish. This crisis was, in its suddenness and scale, really quite unexpected, and its effects – not least higher unemployment and huge public debts – will linger for years to come. Much as we might like to, it won't be possible to go back to "business as usual". Things have changed, and not always in ways we yet fully understand.

The next few years will bring challenges. But, as is often the way, they may also bring opportunities. Perhaps it will be a time when our societies think again about our priorities, about what we really need to achieve with economic growth, and about how we can work with others to tackle shared global problems.

Such opportunities come along rarely. It's a shame to waste them.

Find Out More

OECD

On the Internet

To find out more about OECD work on the individual **BRICS economies**, go to *www.oecd.org/*, and add "China", "India", "Indonesia", "Southafrica", or "Russia" after the slash mark. Specific country and regional coverage is also available at the OECD's Development Centre, *www.oecd.org/DEV*.

For an introduction to OECD work on the **environment**, go to *www.oecd.org/environment*; for "Green Growth", go to *www.oecd.org/greengrowth*.

For an introduction to OECD work on **economics**, go to *www.oecd.org/economics*.

Publications

The Financial Crisis: Reform and Exit Strategies (2009): The financial crisis left major banks crippled by toxic assets and short of capital, while lenders became less willing to finance business and private projects. The immediate and potential impacts on the banking system and the real economy led governments to intervene massively. This book sets out priorities for reforming incentives in financial markets as well as for phasing out these emergency measures.

Making Reform Happen: Lessons from OECD Countries (2010): As governments confront the challenge of trying to restore public finances to health without undermining the recovery, they will need to pursue a careful mix of fiscal policies and growth-enhancing structural reforms. This collection of essays analyses the reform experiences of the 30 OECD countries in nine major policy area in order to identify lessons, pitfalls and strategies that may help foster policy reform.

Perspectives on Global Development – Shifting Wealth (2010): Produced by the OECD's Development Centre, this is the first in a new series of annual outlooks on development issues. This inaugural issue examines the changing dynamics of the global economy over the last 20 years, in particular the impact of the economic rise of large developing countries. It looks also at emerging "south-south" links in areas like foreign direct investment, trade and aid, and ponders their implications for development.

Green Growth: Overcoming the Crisis and Beyond (2009): This discussion paper highlights some of the approaches governments have taken to "green" their recoveries. Available at *www.oecd.org/dataoecd/4/40/43176103. pdf*.

References

Chapter 1

International Monetary Fund (2010), *World Economic Outlook – April 2010*, IMF, Washington, D.C.; *www.imf.org/external/pubs/ft/weo/2010/01/pdf/text.pdf*.

Menschel, R. (2002), *Markets, Mobs & Mayhem*, John Wiley & Sons, Hoboken, N.J.

OECD (2009), *OECD Employment Outlook 2009: Tackling the Jobs Crisis*, OECD Publishing. *http://dx.doi.org/10.1787/empl_outlook-2009-en*

OECD (2010), *OECD Employment Outlook 2010: Moving beyond the Jobs Crisis*, OECD Publishing. *http://dx.doi.org/10.1787/empl_outlook-2010-en*

OECD (2010), *OECD Economic Outlook*, Vol. 2009/2, OECD Publishing. *http://dx.doi.org/10.1787/eco_outlook-v2009-2-en*

OECD (2010), *OECD Factbook 2010: Economic, Environmental and Social Statistics*, OECD Publishing. *http://dx.doi.org/10.1787/factbook-2010-en*

Reinhart, C.M. and K.S. Rogoff (2009), *This Time is Different*, Princeton University Press, Princeton, N.J.

This American Life (2008), "The Giant Pool of Money", Episode No. 355, originally broadcast on 9 May, WBEZ Alliance, Inc.; *www.thisamericanlife.org*.

Tett, G. (2009), *Fool's Gold,* Little, Brown, London.

Vieira, P. (2010), "Q&A with Angel Gurría", 11 June, *National Post*, National Post, Inc., Don Mills, Ontario.

Chapter 2

Blundell-Wignall, A., P. Atkinson and S. Hoon Lee, "The Current Financial Crisis: Causes and Policy Issues", *OECD Journal: Financial Market Trends*, Vol. 2008/2. *http://dx.doi.org/10.1787/fmt-v2008-art10-en*

Blundell-Wignall, A. and P. Atkinson (2008), "The Subprime Crisis: Causal Distortions and Regulatory Reform", in *Lessons from the Financial Turmoil of 2007 and 2008*, proceedings of a conference held at the H.C. Coombs Centre for Financial Studies, Kirribilli, on 14-15 July 2008, Reserve Bank of Australia, Canberra, *www.rba.gov.au/PublicationsAndResearch/Conferences/2008/Blundell-Wignall_Atkinson.pdf.*

Choudhry, M. (2007), *Bank Asset and Liability Management*, John Wiley & Sons, Hoboken, N.J.

Cooper, G. (2008), *The Origin of Financial Crises*, Harriman House Publishing, Petersfield, Hampshire.

Labaton, S. (2008), "Agency's '04 Rule Let Banks Pile Up New Debt", 3 October, *The New York Times*, New York, N.Y.

Morgenson, G. (2007), "Shaky Loans Haunt Mortgages, And Investors, As Crisis Looms", 11 March, *International Herald Tribune*, New York Times Co., New York.

Morgenson, G. (2008), "US Lenders' Attitude: Don't Ask, Don't Tell", 6 April, *International Herald Tribune*, New York Times Co., New York.

Menschel, R. (2002), *Markets, Mobs, and Mayhem*, John Wiley & Sons, Hoboken, N.J.

OECD (2009), *The Financial Crisis: Reform and Exit Strategies*, OECD Publishing, Paris. *http://dx.doi.org/10.1787/9789264073036-en*

Wolf, M. (2009), *Fixing Global Finance*, Yale University Press, New Haven.

Chapter 3

Bhaskaran, M. and R. Ghosh (2010), "Impact and Policy Responses – India," Report No. 3 prepared for the Regional Forum on the Impact of Global Economic and Financial Crisis, 14-15 January, Asian Development Bank, Manila; *www.adb.org/Documents/events/2010/Global-Economic-Financial-Crisis/report-3.pdf.*

Bhaskaran, M. and R. Ghosh (2010), "Impact and Policy Responses – People's Republic of China," Report No. 4 prepared for the Regional Forum on the Impact of Global Economic and Financial Crisis, 14-15 January, Asian Development Bank, Manila; *www.adb.org/Documents/events/2010/Global-Economic-Financial-Crisis/report-4.pdf.*

Bishop, M., (2004), *Essential Economics*, Economist Books/The Economist Newspaper Ltd., London.

Brunnermeier, M.K. (2008), "Deciphering the liquidity and credit crunch 2007-08", NBER Working Paper 14612, National Bureau of Economic Research, Cambridge, MA; *www.nber.org/papers/w14612.*

Dean, A. (2009), "Greece must move quickly on economy", *Kathimerini English Edition*, 12 Oct., I Kathimerini S.A., Athens.

Faulconbridge, G and M. Stott (2009), "Crisis speeds BRIC rise to power: Goldman's O'Neill", 9 June, Thomson Reuters; *www.reuters.com/article/idUSTRE5583ZA20090609.*

Food and Agriculture Organization of the United Nations (2009), *The State of Food Insecurity in the World 2009*, FAO, Rome; accessed at *ftp://ftp.fao.org/docrep/fao/012/i0876e/i0876e.pdf.*

Friedman, J. and N. Schady (2009), "How Many More Infants Are Likely to Die in Africa as a Result of the Global Financial Crisis?", Policy Research Working Paper 5023, August, The World Bank, Washington, D.C.

G-20 (2009), "London Summit – Leaders' Statement", 2 April, accessed at *www.g20.org.*

Hannon, P. (2010), "OECD: Global Government Support For Financial System $11.4 Trillion", Dow Jones Newswires, 13 Jan., News Corp., New York, N.Y.

Haugh, D., P. Ollivaud and D. Turner (2009), "The Macroeconomic Consequences of Banking Crises in OECD Countries", *OECD Economics Department Working Papers*, No.683, OECD, Paris; *http://dx.doi.org/10.1787/226123651438*.

Hemming R., S. Mahfouz and A. Schimmelpfennig (2002), "Fiscal Policy and Economic Activity During Recessions in Advanced Economies", IMF Working Paper WP/02/87, May, International Monetary Fund, Washington, D.C.

Hogg, C. (2009), "Chinese migrant job losses mount", BBC News online, 2 Feb., British Broadcasting Corp., London.

IMF (2009), The Implications of the Global Financial Crisis for Low-Income Countries, March, International Monetary Fund, Washington, D.C.; *www.imf.org/external/pubs/ft/books/2009/globalfin/globalfin.pdf*.

Jiang W. (2009), "Exports see biggest drop in a decade", 12 March, *China Daily*, Beijing; *www.chinadaily.com.cn*.

Kasekende, L., Z. Brixova and L. Ndikumana (2010); "Africa: Africa's Counter-Cyclical Policy", Vol. 1, Issue, 1, *Journal of Globalization and Development*, Berkeley Electronic Press, Berkeley, CA.

O'Brien, C. (2009), "No country for young men", *The Irish Times*, 7 Nov. The Irish Times Ltd., Dublin.

OECD (2008), *OECD Economic Outlook, Vol. 2008/2*, OECD Publishing. *http://dx.doi.org/10.1787/eco_outlook-v2008-2-en*

OECD (2009), *International Migration Outlook: SOPEMI 2009*, OECD Publishing. *http://dx.doi.org/10.1787/migr_outlook-2009-en*

OECD (2009), *OECD Economic Outlook, Vol. 2009/1*, OECD Publishing. *http://dx.doi.org/10.1787/eco_outlook-v2009-1-en*

OECD (2009), *OECD Economic Outlook, Vol. 2009/2*, OECD Publishing. *http://dx.doi.org/10.1787/eco_outlook-v2009-2-en*

OECD (2009), *OECD Employment Outlook 2009: Tackling the Jobs Crisis*, OECD Publishing.
http://dx.doi.org/10.1787/empl_outlook-2009-en

OECD (2009), *OECD Economic Outlook: Interim Report*, March, OECD Publishing.
http://dx.doi.org/10.1787/eco_outlook-v2008-sup2-en

OECD (2009), *OECD Main Economic Indicators (MEI)* database, "Business Tendency and Consumer Opinion Surveys", 6 February 2009,
www.oecd.org/document/4/0,3343,en_2649_33715_42061060_1 _1_1_1,00.html /
http://stats.oecd.org/Index.aspx?DataSetCode=MEI_BTS_COS.

OECD (2009), "The Road to Recovery: Update on the OECD's Strategic Response to the Financial and Economic Crisis", 27 March, OECD, Paris,
www.oecd.org/dataoecd/40/14/42528786.pdf.

OECD (2010), "Donors' mixed aid performance for 2010 sparks concern", 17 Feb., OECD, Paris; *www.oecd.org/dac/stats.*

OECD (2010), *OECD Economic Outlook, Vol. 2010/1*, OECD Publishing. *http://dx.doi.org/10.1787/eco_outlook-v2010-1-en*

OECD (2010), *OECD Employment Outlook 2010: Moving Beyond the Jobs Crisis*, OECD Publishing.
http://dx.doi.org/10.1787/empl_outlook-2010-en

OECD/African Development Bank (2010), *African Economic Outlook 2010*, AfDB/OECD Publishing.
http://dx.doi.org/10.1787/aeo-2010-en

OECD Development Centre (2010), *Perspectives on Global Development 2010: Shifting Wealth*, OECD Publishing.
http://dx.doi.org/10.1787/10.1787/9789264084728-en

Porée, A.-L., (2009) "Cambodia Has to Cope With its Global Connection", Yale Global Online, 11 Aug., Yale Centre for the Study of Globalization, New Haven, CT;
www.yaleglobal.yale.edu.

Postrel, V. (2009), "Macroegonomics", April, *The Atlantic Monthly*, The Atlantic Monthly Group, Washington, D.C.

PricewaterhouseCoopers (2009), "12th Annual Global CEO Survey: Redefining Success"; *www.pwc.com/ceosurvey.*

Randow, J. (2010) "Euro-Area Banks Tighten Credit Standards on Companies, Consumers, ECB Says", 28 July, Bloomberg L.P.; *www.bloomberg.com.*

Ratha, D., S. Mohapatra, and A. Silwal (2009), "Migration and Remittance Trends 2009," *Migration and Development Brief 11,* 3 Nov., World Bank, Washington D.C.; *http://siteresources.worldbank.org/INTPROSPECTS/Resources/ 334934-1110315015165/MigrationAndDevelopmentBrief11.pdf.*

Ravallion, M. (2009), "The Crisis and the World's Poorest", *Development Outreach*, December, World Bank Institute, The World Bank, Washington, D.C.

Reinhart, C.M. and K.S. Rogoff (2009), "The Aftermath of Financial Crises", May, Vol. 99, Issue 2, *American Economic Review*, American Economic Association, Pittsburgh, PA.

Uchitelle, L. (2010), "American Dream Is Elusive for New Generation", 6 Jul., *The New York Times*, The New York Times Co., New York, N.Y.

Wallis, W. (2009), "Africa's aid plea as 'development crisis' looms," 17 March, *Financial Times*, The Financial Times Ltd., London.

World Bank, The (2009), "Swimming Against the Tide: How Developing Countries Are Coping with the Global Crisis", background paper prepared for G20 meeting at Horsham, United Kingdom, 13-14 March, The World Bank, Washington, D.C.; *http://siteresources.worldbank.org/NEWS/Resources/swim mingagainstthetide-march2009.pdf.*

World Bank, The (2009), "Faces of the Crisis: Witaya Rakswong, 37, Bangkok, Thailand", The World Bank, Washington D.C.; *http://go.worldbank.org/SQCPVMN2S0.*

World Bank, The (2009), *Global Economic Prospects 2009: Commodities at the Crossroads*, The International Bank for Reconstruction and Development/The World Bank, Washington, D.C.

World Bank, The (2010), *Global Economic Prospects 2010: Crisis, Finance and Growth*, The International Bank for Reconstruction and Development/The World Bank, Washington, D.C.

Yib C., (2009), "Cambodia's Garment Industry on the Wane", 14 Dec., Deutsche Welle, Bonn; *www.dw-world.de*.

Chapter 4

Keeley, B. (2009), *International Migration: The Human Face of Globalisation*, OECD Insights, OECD Publishing. *http://dx.doi.org/10.1787/9789264055780-en*

OECD (2009), "Helping youth to get a firm foothold in the labour market", background document for the OECD Labour and Employment Ministerial Meeting, 28-29 September, Paris; *www.oecd.org/dataoecd/54/50/43766254.pdf*.

OECD (2009), High-level policy forum on migration website, 29-30 June, *www.oecd.org/migration/policyforum*, accessed 31 March 2010.

OECD (2009), *International Migration Outlook: SOPEMI 2009*, OECD Publishing. *http://dx.doi.org/10.1787/migr_outlook-2009-en*

OECD (2009), "Maintaining the activation stance during the crisis", background document for the OECD Labour and Employment Ministerial Meeting, 28-29 September, Paris; *www.oecd.org/dataoecd/54/48/43766121.pdf*.

OECD (2009), *OECD Employment Outlook: Tackling the Jobs Crisis*, OECD Publishing. *http://dx.doi.org/10.1787/empl_outlook-2009-en*

OECD (2009), OECD Labour and Employment Ministerial Meeting website, *www.oecd.org/employment/ministerial*, accessed 31 March 2010.

OECD (2009), "The Jobs Crisis: What are the implications for employment and social policy?", background document for the OECD Labour and Employment Ministerial Meeting, 28-29 September, Paris; *www.oecd.org/dataoecd/54/62/43765276.pdf*.

Chapter 5

OECD (2009), *Pensions at a Glance 2009: Retirement-Income Systems in OECD Countries*, OECD Publishing. *http://dx.doi.org/10.1787/pension_glance-2009-en*

Antolín, P. and F. Stewart (2009), "Private Pensions and Policy Responses to the Financial and Economic Crisis", *OECD Journal: Financial Market Trends*, Vol. 2009/1, No. 36, OECD Publishing. *http://dx.doi.org/10.1787/fmt-v2009-art5-en*

Bank of England (2009), "Provisional estimates of narrow money (notes & coin) and reserve balances", *www.bankofengland.co.uk/statistics/nc/current/index.htm.*

Clark, N. (2009), "RBS plans to slash pension payout as unions cry foul", *The Independent*, 26 August.

Deloitte (2009), "Quantitative easing contributes to FTSE 100 pension scheme deficits increasing to £180bn", 8 April 2009, *www.deloitte.com/view/en_GB/uk/press-release/4a140b98fc001210VgnVCM100000ba42f00aRCRD.htm.*

Financial Times (2010), "The Pensions Crisis", *www.ft.com/indepth/pensions-crisis.*

Helm, T. and P. Inman (2009), "Pensions blow for those soon to retire: New OAPs to be hit by 'quantitative easing'", *The Observer*, 29 March.

Keith, T. (2009), "Pension Woes May Deepen Financial Crisis For States", NPR, 21 March 2010, *www.npr.org/templates/story/story.php?storyId=124894618.*

Mangiero, S. (2010), *Negative Swap Spreads - Trouble On the Way?, Pension Risk Matters*, 12 April, *www.pensionriskmatters.com/2010/04/articles/asset-liability-management/negative-swap-spreads-trouble-on-the-way.*

OECD (2008), *Improving Financial Education and Awareness on Insurance and Private Pensions*, OECD Publishing. *http://dx.doi.org/10.1787/9789264046399-en*

OECD (2009), *OECD Private Pensions Outlook*, OECD Publishing. *http://dx.doi.org/10.1787/9789264044395-en*

OECD (2009), *The Political Economy of Reform: Lessons from Pensions, Product Markets and Labour Markets in Ten OECD Countries*, OECD Publishing. *http://dx.doi.org/10.1787/9789264073111-en*

Chapter 6

Blundell-Wignall, A., P. Atkinson and S.H. Lee (2008), "The Current Financial Crisis: Causes and Policy Issues," *OECD Journal: Financial Market Trends*, Vol. 2008/2, OECD Publishing. *http://dx.doi.org/10.1787/fmt-v2008-art10-en*

Blundell-Wignall, A. and P. Atkinson (2009), "Origins of the Financial Crisis and Requirements for Reform", *Journal of Asian Economics*, Elsevier; *http://dx.doi.org/10.1016/j.asieco.2009.07.009*

Blundell-Wignall, A., G. Wehinger and P. Slovik (2009) "The Elephant in the Room: The Need to Deal with What Banks Do", *OECD Journal: Financial Market Trends*, Vol. 2009/2, OECD Publishing. *http://dx.doi.org/10.1787/fmt-v2009-art11-en*

Borio, C., C. Furfine and P. Lowe (2001), "Procyclicality of the Financial System and Financial Stability: Issues and Policy Options", March, BIS Papers No. 1, Bank for International Settlements, Basel; *www.bis.org/publ/bppdf/bispap01a.pdf.*

Brown, G. (2009), "Speech and Q&A at St Paul's Cathedral", 31 Mar., at St Paul's Cathedral, London; *www.number10.gov.uk.*

Cassidy, J. (2009), *How Markets Fail: The Logic of Economic Calamities*, Farrar, Straus and Giroux, New York, N.Y.

Christian Aid (2008), "Death And Taxes: The True Toll Of Tax Dodging – A Christian Aid Report", *www.christianaid.org.uk/images/deathandtaxes.pdf.*

Cooper, G. (2008), *The Origins of Financial Crises*, Harriman House Ltd., London.

Davis, B. (2009), "'Framework' precedents", 25 September, *The Wall Street Journal*, Dow Jones & Co. Inc., New York, NY.

Dougherty C. (2008), "Top German CEO steps down as tax scandal widens to 'several hundred people'," 5 Nov., *International Herald Tribune*, New York Times Co., New York.

Economist, The, "Economics A–Z",
   www.economist.com/research/economics.

Economist, The (2010), "Not all on the same page", 1 Jul., *The Economist*, The Economist Newspaper Ltd., London.

Financial Stability Board (2009), "Improving Financial Regulation: Report of the Financial Stability Board to G20 Leaders", paper presented at Pittsburgh summit, 25 Sep.; *www.financialstabilityboard.org/publications/r_090925b.pdf.*

GlobeScan/PIPA/BBC World Service (2009), "Wide Dissatisfaction with Capitalism — Twenty Years after Fall of Berlin Wall", 9 Nov., GlobeScan, Toronto; *www.globescan.com.*

Grant, J. and M. Mackenzie (2010), "Ghosts in the machine", *Financial Times*, 17 Feb, The Financial Times Ltd, London.

G20 (2009), "Leaders Statement: The Global Plan for Recovery and Reform – London, 2 April 2009", *www.g20.org/Documents/final-communique.pdf.*

G20 (2009), "Leaders' Statement: The Pittsburgh Summit", statement released in Washington, D.C., 24-25 Sept.; *www.pittsburghsummit.gov/mediacenter/129639.htm.*

Gurría, A. (2008), "The Global Dodgers", 27 Nov., *The Guardian*, Guardian News and Media Ltd., London.

Gurría, A. (2008), "Tax disclosures in Germany part of a broader challenge, says OECD Secretary-General," 19 Feb., OECD, Paris, *www.oecd.org/document/34/0,3343,en_2649_201185_40114018_1_1_1_1,00.html.*

Gurría, A. (2009), "The Need for a Global Standard", speech by OECD Secretary-General A. Gurría, delivered at the G7 Finance Ministers Dinner in Rome, 13 Feb., OECD; *www.oecd.org/document/50/0,3343,en_2649_34487_42184370_1_1_1_1,00.html.*

Haldane, A.G. and P. Alessandri (2009), "Banking on the state", *BIS Review*, Bank for International Settlements, Basel; *www.bis.org/review/r091111e.pdf.*

Hay, G. And L. Silva Laughlin (2009), "How Living Wills Could Help Banks", 15 Sep., *The New York Times*, The New York Times Co., New York, N.Y.

Jolly, D. (2009), "2 Nations Agree to Ease Bank Secrecy Rules," *International Herald Tribune*, 12 Mar., New York Times Co., New York.

Kaiser, E. (2008), "After AIG rescue, Fed may find more at its door", 17 Sep., Reuters; *www.reuters.com/article/idUKN1644235820080917*.

Kirkpatrick, G. (2009), "Corporate Governance Lessons from the Financial Crisis", *OECD Journal: Financial Market Trends*, Vol. 2009/1, OECD Publishing. *http://dx.doi.org/10.1787/fmt-v2009-art3-en*

Marcussen, M. (2005), "The OECD: Soft Regulation and Solid Reputation", Paper presented at annual meeting of International Studies Association, 5 Mar., Honolulu, HI.

Mazzoni, A. (2009), "The 'Lecce Framework' and 'Soft Law'", The Global Standard Blog, 16 Jul, OECD; *https://community.oecd.org/community/gcls/blog/2009/07/16/the-lecce-framework-and-soft-law*.

Merkel, A. and J.P. Balkenende (2009), "Values for a Sustainable World Economy", 19 Mar., *Spiegel Online*; *www.spiegel.de/international/world/0,1518,614251,00.html*.

Obama, B. (2009), "Remarks by the President on Financial Rescue and Reform", 14 Sep. at Federal Hall, New York, N.Y.; *www.whitehouse.gov*.

OECD (2006), "Policy Brief on Corporate Governance of Banks in Asia", June, from the Asian Roundtable on Corporate Governance, OECD, Paris; *www.oecd.org/dataoecd/48/55/37180641.pdf*.

OECD (2009), "Policy Framework for Effective and Efficient Financial Regulation", 3 Dec., OECD, Paris; *www.oecd.org/dataoecd/24/53/42221702.pdf*.

OECD (2009), *The Financial Crisis: Reform and Exit Strategies*, OECD Publishing. *http://dx.doi.org/10.1787/9789264073036-en*

OECD (2009), *Government at a Glance 2009*, OECD Publishing. *http://dx.doi.org/10.1787/9789264075061-en*

OECD (2009), "OECD Economic Outlook No. 85", *OECD Economic Outlook: Statistics and Projections* (database). *http://dx.doi.org/10.1787/data-00367-en*

OECD (2009), *OECD's Current Tax Agenda – September 2009*, OECD, Paris; *www.oecd.org/dataoecd/38/17/1909369.pdf.*

OECD (2009), "Countering Offshore Tax Evasion: Some Questions and Answers", 28 September, OECD, Paris; *www.oecd.org/dataoecd/23/13/42469606.pdf.*

OECD Observer (2010), "What Banks Actually Do", Dec. 2009-Jan. 2010, *OECD Observer*, OECD, Paris.

O'Toole, F. (2010), "Balancing profit and loss, ups and downs, right and wrong", 6 Mar., *The Irish Times*, The Irish Times Ltd., Dublin.

Reuters (2009), "G20 Final Communiqué–Annex: Sustainable Growth", 25 Sep.,; *www.reuters.com/article/idUSTRE58O6W520090925.*

Solow, R.M. (2010), "Hedging America", *The New Republic*, 12 Jan., The New Republic, Washington, D.C.

Tett, G. (2009), *Fool's Gold*, Little, Brown, London.

Treanor, J. (2010), "Even my parents think I'm overpaid, admits RBS chief executive", 12 Jan., *The Guardian*, Guardian News and Media Ltd., London.

Wall Street Journal, The (2009), "Volcker: Be Bold," 14 Dec., *The Wall Street Journal*, Dow Jones & Co., New York, N.Y.

Valaskakis, K. (2009), "Are 'Frameworks' and 'Guidelines' Sufficient?", The Global Standard Blog, 27 Jul., OECD; *https://community.oecd.org/community/gcls/blog/2009/07/27/ are-frameworks-and-guidelines-sufficient.*

Wheatcroft, P. (2009), "City Shouldn't Rise to Sarkozy Rhetoric", 3 Dec., *The Wall Street Journal*, Dow Jones & Co. Inc., New York, NY.

White, W.R. (2010), "Is financial stability enough", No 276-277, Dec. 2009-Jan. 2010, *OECD Observer*, OECD Publishing; *www.oecdobserver.org/news/fullstory.php/aid/3137*

Chapter 7

Benhaim, F. and R. Clarke (2009), "The green growth race", Jun. 2009, No. 273, *OECD Observer*, OECD, Paris; *www.oecdobserver.org/news/fullstory.php/aid/2928/The_green_growth_race.html*.

Cassidy, J. (2008), "He Foresaw the End of an Era", 23 Oct., The New York Review of Books, NYREV, Inc., New York, N.Y.; *www.nybooks.com/articles/archives/2008/oct/23/he-foresaw-the-end-of-an-era*.

Cecchetti, S., M. Mohanty and F. Zampolli (2010), "The future of public debt: prospects and implications", BIS Working Paper No. 300, Bank for International Settlements, Berne; *www.bis.org/publ/work300.pdf?noframes=1*.

Cooper, G. (2008), *The Origins of Financial Crises*, Harriman House Ltd., London.

Cukier, J. (2010), "Deepening Debt", *OECD Factblog*, OECD Publishing, *https://community.oecd.org/community/factblog/blog/2010/03/23/deepening-debt*.

Daily Telegraph, The (2009), "Queen told how economists missed financial crisis", 26 Jul., *The Daily Telegraph*, Telegraph Media Group Ltd., London, *www.telegraph.co.uk/news/newstopics/theroyalfamily/5912697/Queen-told-how-economists-missed-financial-crisis.html*.

Economist, The (2009), "The Other-Worldly Philosophers", 18 Jul., *The Economist*, The Economist Newspaper Ltd., London.

Frondel, M. *et al.* (2009), "Economic Impacts from the Promotion of Renewable Energy Technologies: The German Experience", Ruhr Economic Papers #156, Rheinisch-Westfälisches Institut für Wirtschaftsforschung (RWI), Essen; *http://en.rwi-essen.de/media/content/pages/publikationen/ruhr-economic-papers/REP_09_156.pdf*.

Gurría, A. (2009), "The Korean G-20 leadership: Assessing the key issues for 2010 – New sources of sustainable and balanced growth", remarks by the Secretary General of the OECD in Seoul, 17 Nov.; *www.oecd.org/document/18/0,3343,en_2649_37465_44080146_1_1_1_1,00.html*.

Gurría, A. (2010), "The transformation of China's growth pattern in the new global context", Speech by the Secretary General of the OECD at the China Development Forum in Beijing on 20 Mar., *www.oecd.org/document/32/0,3343,en_2649_34487_44848288_1_1_1_1,00.html*.

Hankinson, A. (2010), "How graduates are picking up the tab for their parents' lives", 31 Jan., *The Guardian*, Guardian News and Media Ltd., London.

International Monetary Fund (2009), *World Economic Outlook 2009*, IMF, Washington D.C.; *www.imf.org/external/pubs/ft/weo/2009/01/index.htm*.

International Monetary Fund (2010), *World Economic Outlook 2010*, IMF, Washington D.C.; *www.imf.org/external/pubs/ft/weo/2010/update/01/pdf/0110.pdf*.

Kaletsky, A. (2010) "Academics ready to crush old economic theories with a new reality", 6 Apr., *The Times*, News Corp., London.

Keegan, W. (2009), "The sad truth is, Your Majesty, we banked on this never happening", 22 Feb., *The Observer*, Guardian News and Media Ltd., London, *www.guardian.co.uk/business/2009/feb/22/bankers-criticism-credit-crunch*.

Krugman, P. (2010), "The Pain Caucus", 30 May., *The New York Times*, The New York Times Co., New York, N.Y.

Kwok, V.W.-Y. (2009), "Weaknesses in Chinese Wind Power", 20 Jun., *Forbes Asia*, Forbes, New York, N.Y.

Love, P. (2010), "OECD Economic Outlook: 'Disconnected from real needs'?", 2 Jun., OECD Insights Blog; *http://oecdinsights.org/2010/06/02/oecd-economic-outlook-disconnected-from-real-needs/*.

Mihm, S. (2008), "Dr. Doom", 15 Aug., *The New York Times*, The New York Times Co., New York, N.Y.

OECD (2009), *Highlights from Education at a Glance 2009*, OECD Publishing.
http://dx.doi.org/10.1787/eag_highlights-2009-en

OECD (2009), OECD Factbook 2009: Economic, Environmental and Social Statistics, OECD Publishing.
http://dx.doi.org/10.1787/factbook-2009-en

OECD (2009), *The Economics of Climate Change Mitigation: Policies and Options for Global Action beyond 2012*, OECD Publishing.
http://dx.doi.org/10.1787/9789264073616-en

OECD (2009), *The Financial Crisis: Reform and Exit Strategies*, OECD Publishing.
http://dx.doi.org/10.1787/9789264073036-en

OECD (2010), *Economic Policy Reforms: Going for Growth 2010*, OECD Publishing.
http://dx.doi.org/10.1787/growth-2010-en

OECD (2010),"OECD Economic Outlook No. 86", *OECD Economic Outlook: Statistics and Projections* (database), accessed on 2/17/2010. *http://dx.doi.org/10.1787/data-00370-en*

OECD (2010), *OECD Economic Outlook*, Vol. 2009/2, OECD Publishing. *http://dx.doi.org/10.1787/eco_outlook-v2009-2-en*

OECD (n.d.), "Preparing Fiscal Consolidation", Economics Department, OECD, Paris;
www.oecd.org/dataoecd/16/1/44829122.pdf

OECD (2010), *Interim Report of the Green Growth Strategy: Implementing our Commitment for a Sustainable Future, report prepared for Meeting of the OECD Council at Ministerial Level*, 27-28 May 2010;
www.oecd.org/dataoecd/42/46/45312720.pdf

OECD Development Centre (2010), *Perspectives on Global Development 2010: Shifting Wealth*, OECD Publishing.
http://dx.doi.org/10.1787/10.1787/9789264084728-en

Schwartz, N.D. and M. Saltmarsh (2009), "Developing World Seen as Engine for Recovery", 25 Jun., *The New York Times*, New York Times Co., New York, N.Y.

Seager, A. (2010), "Beware global economic imbalances, Mervyn King warns", 20 Jan., *The Guardian*, Guardian News and Media Ltd., London.

Skidelsky, R. and M. Miller (2010), "Do not rush to switch off the life support", 4 Mar., *The Financial Times*, The Financial Times Limited, London.

Taleb, N.N. (2008), *The Black Swan: The Impact of the Highly Improbable*, Penguin Books, London.

United Nations Framework Convention on Climate Change (2007), "Climate Change: Impacts, Vulnerabilities and Adaptation in Developing Countries", UNFCCC, Bonn; *http://unfccc.int/resource/docs/publications/impacts.pdf*.

Walker, M and C. Forelle (2010), "Euro-Zone Leaders Seek Compromise on Aid for Greece", *The Wall Street Journal*, Dow Jones & Co., New York.

Walker, M. (2010), "Economies hinge on exit strategies", 25 Jan., *The Wall Street Journal*, Dow Jones & Co., New York.

White, W. (2009), "Modern Macroeconomics is on the Wrong Track", Dec., Finance & Development, International Monetary Fund, Washington D.C.; *www.imf.org/external/pubs/ft/fandd/2009/12/pdf/white.pdf*.

Wolf, M. (2010), "The long road ahead", 11 Feb., *The Financial Times*, The Financial Times Limited, London.

Photo credits:

OECD PUBLISHING, 2, rue André-Pascal, 75775 PARIS CEDEX 16
PRINTED IN FRANCE
(01 2010 07 1 P) ISBN 978-92-64-06911-4 – No. 57099 2010

DATE DUE